The Next Chapter

*Stories Told through
the Rearview Mirror*

BOB CRAIG

CLAY BRIDGES
PRESS

The Next Chapter
Stories Told through the Rearview Mirror

Published by Clay Bridges in Houston, TX
www.ClayBridgesPress.com

Scripture quotations are taken from the New American Standard Bible® (NASB), Copyright © 1960, 1962, 1963, 1968, 1971, 1972, 1973, 1975, 1977, 1995 by The Lockman Foundation. Used by permission. www.Lockman.org.

ISBN-10: 1-939815-40-1
ISBN-13: 978-1-939815-40-8
eISBN-10: 1-939815-41-X
eISBN-13: 978-1-939815-41-5

Special Sales: Most Clay Bridges titles are available in special quantity discounts. Custom imprinting or excerpting can also be done to fit special needs. Contact Clay Bridges at Info@ClayBridgesPress.com.

Table of Contents

Preface

The cars I have owned, or at least made payments on, have served as chapters in my life. In this book, I have noted some of the significant events that I can recall from the times each car was in our use. None of the chapters are exhaustive. Each is limited by the accuracy of an aging memory. Taken together, these chapters form a sketchy history of the life of our immediate family.

I have had a hard time getting comfortable with cars. As you will note as we proceed through the following pages, I have dabbled too much with too great a variety of cars. However, that dabbling gives me a convenient way of telling about some events that are my life. You may want to shake your head in wonder that I took so long to settle this issue about automobiles.

The first chapter, "1946 Chevrolet Van," will start with the Craig family's move from Missouri to Texas. Each chapter is a witness of grace. My mismanagement of time and budget could have—should have—entitled more penalty than grace. There are instances of which I am not proud. There are instances of which I am humbled. In it all, these chapters are a recording of a life that has been rescued and is being delivered by the awesome grace of God.

My hope is that anyone who reads these chapters will be more than entertained—they will be blessed and encouraged.

1946 Chevrolet Van

I was nine years old when we packed what we could into this paneled van. As you read, you have to remember that these events happened in the life of a young person as recalled by that person when he was much older. Details might be fuzzy, but not intentionally.

We came to Texas, as I recall, to find work. Daddy had worked earlier at what was then the Humble Refinery in Baytown (at that time called the "Tri-Cities"). Without a house to move into, we rented rooms at the Pelly Courts, a motel in Pelly—one of the Tri-Cities.

Before too long (I warned you that an old memory is trying to work here), we moved into a grocery store—in the front—with housing in the back. There was a screen door on the grocery side, with an advertisement for Rainbow Bread. I don't remember us ever operating that grocery store.

I do remember a time when we stopped by there while some other party was running the store. We ordered a pound of bologna. Without a slicing machine, the clerk cut the meat by hand and eye. In those days, lunch meat came in loaves—rounded or rectangular. We got three slices of lunch meat that added up to a pound! Started thin, and ended up not so thin.

I remember helping Mother make bedsteads out of the bread racks (since they were no longer needed, as we weren't selling any groceries). Mother was always quite handy, and would tackle any job. As we were dismantling the racks, I remember Mother busting her shin as the hammer bounced off the wood.

The chronology might be incorrect, but some really interesting things happened in this chapter of our lives.

There were two large buildings on the property where we were living. Above us were two apartments. Beside and behind us was the other building. Mr. and Mrs. Airhart lived on the bottom floor. I suppose someone lived upstairs.

Somehow, I got a BB gun. I'd had a single-shot 22 when we still lived in Missouri, and I fancied myself as a great white hunter. This BB gun gave me a chance to exercise my abilities now that we were in Texas. It was not that good of a gun. In fact, if you held it with the barrel pointing down, the BBs would roll out. I attempted to shoot a bird with this wimpy gun. It must have been one of those birds that prefers running along the ground to flying. I spotted him coming out from under Mrs. Airhart's house—I preferred not to think I might have been depriving a chirper of its mother. With a fresh BB in the barrel, I aimed down to shoot. . .and the BB rolled out! I made enough noise that the bird ran back under the house. To his surprise and mine, he came out on the other side. I reloaded, with the same results. I can't remember which of us finally gave it up. The bird was unharmed—although possibly winded. I was disgusted with my gun.

There was a railroad that ran almost over our house—we were that close to the track. The railbed had been elevated to allow drainage and to encourage traffic to slow down as it approached the crossing (that delay has an important impact on following events). Under the tracks was a heavily constructed ditch. Totally without permission, we would sit in that ditch while the train was crossing. What noise and dust! Yes, we should have known better. No, Mother did not know.

Mother did know, however, about the little ponds that were created when the railbed was being built. We were strongly (maybe not a strong enough word) instructed to not get into those ponds. There were clams that bedded into the wet banks. We would dig one out, cut it open, and use it to bait hooks (usually made by bending straight pins) and fish. Nothing we ever caught was worth keeping. Of course, being that close to the water was irresistible, and we would dive in. We would walk the mile or so back home, hoping the wind would dry our hair so that Mother wouldn't know that we had defied her orders. Never did fool her.

The railroad ran into town. Those were the "good old days" when a dime (yes, a dime!) would get you into the Saturday matinee. For that dime, we got to see two features (usually some cowboy hero), a serial (usually some sci-fi), and a comedy—and get one cent back in change! Woolworth was close to the theater, so that one cent could be used. The walk to town was filled with anticipation. The walk home, with reviews.

There were deep drainage ditches on both sides of Cedar Bayou Road. When it would rain—which seemed often in what was soon named "Baytown"—we would fish for crawdads. A piece of kite string, a nail (for weight), and a piece of fat bacon equipped a crawfisherman. In a good day when we would fish until our bait was consumed, we could fill the bottom of a wash tub. With a good deal of coaxing (translate that as "begging"), Mother would fry up the tails that we cleaned.

Robyn and I went to Cedar Bayou Elementary (the others, Randy and Richey, were not yet school age). As I remember it, the bus stopped just at our door before the railroad crossing.

I started my band career at Cedar Bayou. I can't recall where we got that trumpet that I started on. Honestly, that mouthpiece was too small for my big mouth. After we moved, Mr. Parker moved me to baritone—and then to bass horn.

I attempted to make the football team, despite the fact that I was a runt. I can't recall much, but I do remember Coach Davis challenging us during drills. We were doing push-ups. Coach said, "Do all you can. . .then one more." I escaped football without any injury.

Remember I said something about the impact of that railroad crossing? Cars couldn't cross it without slowing down. One day, Gerry Kelly was driving our direction down Cedar Bayou Road. Robyn happened to be playing out in the yard. We didn't know it then, but Mrs. Kelly taught girls Robyn's age in Sunday School at Stewart Heights Baptist Church. She pulled her car into our lot, and introduced herself to Mother. She asked if she could stop by and take Robyn to Sunday School, since she taught girls that age. Mother, being a mother, said that Robyn wasn't dressed properly, but, if Mrs. Kelly would stop by next week, Robyn would be ready to go to Sunday School with her.

Mother used that "bigger brother" thing on me. Robyn couldn't go by herself. It was my duty, as big brother, to go with her. We were ready when Mrs. Kelly came the next Sunday. Our lives, family included, took a much different direction from that Sunday on.

Robyn and I loved Sunday School. The church just adopted us. We decided that we could walk the short distance from where we lived to church. We became evangelists, begging Mother to come to church with us. It didn't happen all at once, if I remember correctly. Sis and I would walk along Cedar Bayou Road, then cross the ditch, cut through Mrs. Wolfe's yard, and arrive at church.

The Kellys had a son close to my age and a daughter close to Robyn's. Our social life picked up—for the better.

Eddie Albright became a special mentor for me. Eddie was a plumber, with "Popeye arms." I marveled at his strength—and his willingness to let me help him. He trusted me to thread pipe, to tamp molted lead (it was ok at that time) into the joints of cast-iron pipe. He even let me help him dig the ditches to bury pipe. I must have bugged him, but he never let on.

Gordon Albright had a beautiful wife that I fell in love with. She was kind to me.

I don't know what happened to that '46 Chevrolet Panel Van. For some time, we were without a car. Daddy would take the bus to and from work. Daddy never shied from any work. He was very dedicated to his family and would do whatever he had to do to care for us. For too long, Daddy had allowed himself to be influenced by a drinking habit. Despite that, Daddy cared for his family.

Somehow—I was too young then to be aware of the details—we got a house in Morrell Park: 404 Morrell Street became our new address. Let this change of address lead us into our next chapter.

1946 Chevrolet Sedan

I don't know how we moved from Cedar Bayou Road to Morrell Park. We didn't have a car of our own. I suppose volunteers from Stewart Heights helped us (remember, I was young so likely not in the know, and I am old now with that accompanying memory). However it happened, it was bliss.

We were now in a neighborhood. There were five houses on our side of the block. Nearly all the houses were built alike—same floor plan, same elevation. The house was a square with enough driveway poured that a skillful driver could straddle the lanes. Each drive led to a detached garage. There was one bath, two bedrooms (we had three boys and Robyn), and a kitchen large enough to eat in. The backyard was fenced with chain-link fencing. Across the back of the yard was the clothesline. It was a four-wire model.

Somehow, in the move, Daddy had landed a job with Higgenbotham Motors, as a salesman. Ever since we had been introduced to the folks at Stewart Heights Baptist Church, we had been begging Daddy to come to church with us. As earlier noted, Daddy was a proud man. He wouldn't go to church until he could take his family in a car with him.

We wouldn't give up on him. Eventually, Daddy said that when he got a car so that we wouldn't have to "beg a ride," he would go with us to church. As he was getting ready to go to the bus stop on a Saturday evening, the boss said, "Just take one of our cars for over the weekend. You will be back here Monday morning." Now, Daddy had a car so that he wouldn't have to ask for a ride. When he drove in, we met him at the drive. "Remember what you told us," we reminded him. Daddy kept his word, and for the first time I can remember, our family went together to church.

Mother and I sang in our little choir. Mr. Lindstrum was patient in teaching me to sing bass with him. I could read music from my band experience. Mother was an exceptional alto. Brother Smith was our pastor. Each of our Sunday services ended with an invitation to acknowledge a commitment to Christ. To my delighted surprise, Daddy came to the front to take Brother Smith's hand and announce that he was giving his life to Christ! I have a copy of the testimony Daddy later wrote—in his own hand—to share in witnessing. That testimony reads:

> I was 37 years old when I was saved. It was at a small church (Stewart Heights). I had been an awful sinner, but God had mercy and love for me. A great peace came over me after many tears of repentance. That was the greatest event of my life. Even now, I'm thankful daily for this great salvation from God.

Our little family had been struggling to survive. Daddy worked hard, but drinking is very expensive. I recall sometimes when we would receive Thanksgiving baskets in season. Generous people at church would give us usable things. From the day that Daddy united his family in commitment to God, our fortunes took an upward swing.

An indication of our "fortune" was the purchase (from Mr. Lewis, I think) of a 1946 Chevrolet Sedan. As I recall, it was an industrial blue. It was a two-door, six-cylinder, with an innovation Chevrolet called "vacuum shift." That innovation was designed to siphon off vacuum from the manifold and ease the shifting of gears in the manual transmission.

Those Chevrolets were notoriously "cold-natured." Until the engine warmed up, you had to choke it. Nowadays, that is automatic. Then, you had to pull out a knob that would close down the fly in the carburetor giving you a richer fuel mixture. The designers of that model had put the choke knob next to the tuner for the radio—making the driver reach almost into the passenger's seat to reach the knob.

Mother taught me to drive in that car. It was Mother because Daddy was always at work, across town. I can't count the times when the car would attempt to stall because of that cold engine, and Mother would pull out the radio tuning knob in her efforts to choke the car.

With "four on the column," I had to learn the coordination of clutch and shifting. It was not pretty. The shifting was an H-pattern. First was on the H, in and down. Second was up and out. Third, which you drove in, was straight down from second. Reverse was on the H, up and in. Countless times, as I was learning, I went from first to reverse. Not pretty. Chevrolets are tough, and ours survived my abuse.

Not long after we got Mr. Lewis's old car, we were hit on the passenger-side door. The damage was not worth the price of repair, so we learned to live with it. That door could never be trusted to stay closed. When I was allowed to drive it on dates, that unreliable door became a very useful means of getting the girl to sit closer to me.

During the time we had that '46 Chevy Sedan, we had memorable adventures at 404 Morrell. Rodney and Reggie were born while we lived in Morrell Park.

With our boys so far outnumbering the girls—and having only two bedrooms in the house—Mother decided (she had always been creative, and shied from no challenge) to convert our garage into "The Boy's House." We sheet-rocked the walls, and made a closet and a built-in chest of drawers. We moved beds into "The Boy's House" and moved us out of the main house.

Our lives were being changed by our fellowship in Stewart Heights Baptist Church. In those days, a "good Baptist" didn't go to the picture show. Television was in the same classification as dancing. We enjoyed watching TV (guilty pleasure?), but had to go to neighbor's houses to do so. We were coming out of our economic hole since money wasn't being wasted on alcohol. Our family decided to purchase a television set. Of course, we could not have such a demonic instrument in our house, so we installed it in "The Boy's House." Our consciences were soothed, and we didn't have to go next door to watch wrestling on Friday nights.

Maybe it was the first Christmas we celebrated at 404 Morrell that we got our basketball and goal. Rodney was just walking and talking. Montgomery Wards was our "Santa Claus," and Robyn and I were helping Santa.

7

We had hidden the gifts in the attic. How surprised we were when we saw Rodney standing under the door of the attic pointing up and saying, "Ball!"

We built a backboard for the goal, and mounted it on the back of "The Boy's House" (other folks' garage). A real proof—and test—of ability was to be able to make a shot over the clothesline. Both Mother and Daddy utilized that old two-handed push shot, but they were quite deadly with it. There was no need to mow behind "The Boy's House" because we kept the grass beaten down with our basketball.

The move to Morrell Park put us in another school district. I went to Horace Mann Junior High. I was still a runt. I did attempt football, but settled on band instead. I was quite hot on the bass horn. More than one time, Mr. Parker instructed me to put my mouthpiece into my pocket. I couldn't resist blasting.

Each day at Horace Mann began with a playing of "Call to the Colors." Each room would stand while the "Call" was being played. Then, we would recite the pledge to the flag. Someone would voice a prayer over the address system. Only then would class work begin.

Tennis was really big in those days. Addiction to tennis brought me the grief of my most memorable discipling. It became fashionable to wear "church clothes" to school. I did have a favorite pair of slacks. I had a tennis racket, and waited (as others did) for a turn on one of the several courts at the school.

Do schools still have an occasional period when class is dismissed so that the teachers can meet? During one of those times, I used the early dismissal as an opportunity to play more tennis. Mother didn't need to know. I would get home at the normal time. So, with my Sunday pants on, I engaged in a competitive game of tennis. Time flew by as we contested game after game. What time was it, anyway?

Our old Chevrolet needed shocks—badly. When you hit a bump, you would bounce into the next bump. I knew I was in trouble when I saw the Chevy bumping across the railroad tracks that bordered the courts. My opponent had just returned with a high lob that I had to run back to return. My attention was diverted (too soft a word) by that bouncing Chevrolet, and I fell on the court—busting the knee out of my best pants.

Mother was sadistically calm. Without raising her voice, she asked why I hadn't come home as she expected. Then, coldly, she informed me that I would be getting a whipping when we got home. Past experiences caused my heart to sink. As if a part of my suffering, Mother took a longer route home. She even stopped to visit Mrs. Lilly about some Women's Missionary Union business—leaving me to suffer in the car (mothers seem to do that, leave kids waiting in the car while they do business). There was never any consideration that she would forget what she had promised me.

We finally got home. Beside the front door was a Ligustrum. The limbs were long and flexible—like a whip. I had the privilege of choosing the weapon that would drive addiction out of my mind. Mother knew how to leave just enough of the foliage on the limb. In her hands, that Ligustrum limb was a lethal weapon.

To my best memory (from then to now), that was my last whipping. It was a classic.

The Marshalls lived next door. They had a beautiful little daughter about the same age as Rodney. On the other side of our house were the Sanders. Their son was Gary. I was shooting baskets in our backyard and could see Gary and Marilyn playing in the sandpile in Marshall's backyard. Lying between them was Pal, a German Shepherd. Suddenly, without any warning or apparent provocation, Pal took Gary's face into his mouth! I jumped over the fence and grabbed Gary to run to his house. His little face was a bloody mess. Of course, Mrs. Marshall could scarcely believe that her pet would do such a thing. I don't remember what they did with Pal. Gary recovered. It was one of those indelible experiences that won't go away.

We played baseball in the backyard. If you hit it over the fence, it was an automatic out. We had one base. First (and only) base was the clothesline. Our bat was an oak limb (about the right size) with a handle whittled out. We played football in the street. The curbs in front of the neighbors' yards were the out-of-bounds markers. Oncoming cars meant a temporary delay as we cleared the street.

Moore's Grocery was on the corner of the block just down from ours. Back then, you could buy on weekly credit. We had a pad, with carbons, that Mrs. Moore used to record our purchases. When Daddy got his check, we would go and pay what the pad had listed.

The store had a galvanized tin roof. In the evenings, after closing, we would contest one another in attempts to hit a walnut (know how hard they are?) with a baseball bat to bounce off the roof of Moore's store.

It would rain often and hard in Morrell Park. Drainage was poor. We were forbidden to play in the standing water (Mother seemed to think it wasn't healthy). After one of those frequent rains, water was standing at the corner where the Guests lived. Just as we rounded the corner to come home, we saw Rodney doing a "preacher's seat" (some called it a cannonball) into the standing water. Mother was not amused, even when Rodney said, "I slipped and fell."

Housing developments ended up at Garth Road. That undeveloped area became our "jungle." We spent hours there. We would vault across a little creek. We would combat imaginary foes. We made fun.

We got our first gas-powered mower during this time. Yep, we brought it home in that 1946 Chevrolet. We got the mower at Sears. It was a two-cycle, which meant that we had to mix the gas and oil. Mother thought we could make some money mowing other people's yards. We did get Mrs. Roden's yard. Hers was not a gift.

Mrs. Roden lived beside the Interurban tracks in old Baytown. Her yard was a handy receptacle for cans and beer bottles. We may have been the very first to attempt to mow that portion of her yard. It was a full day's work—for $5.

The mower proved to be as much for aerobic exercise (pulling the starting cord) as for mowing.

I graduated into Robert E. Lee High School while we were still driving that '46 Chevy. There were more than several kids in our neighborhood who were also in the band. Rather than ride the bus (which would leave for home while we were yet rehearsing), we made up a car pool. When it was my turn to drive, I always had to warn the passenger about that uncertain door.

Sometime after we moved into 404 Morrell, we got a piano. I think it was Mother's hope that Robyn would catch onto the piano. She did try. So did I. However, it was a perfect fit for Richey. "Like a fish to water" is a poor analogy to how Richey took to the piano. Practice was no chore for him. His big hands never had any trouble hitting the right keys. We found that he could play from a score and could play by ear. The piano really opened life for Richey. Only heaven will reveal how many lives have been blessed by his use of the talent and ability God gave him. We did a small bit in getting that old upright piano.

In my junior year at Lee, we got the first new car I can remember. Daddy came home with a 1954 Ford Station Wagon. With three seats, it would seat nine—which seemed proper for our family.

That 1954 Ford ushered in the next chapter.

1954 Ford Station Wagon

I can't remember what happened with our old faithful '46 Chevrolet. It had served us well. It was the chariot in which I learned to drive. How I got my license is an interesting story.

In my day, you had to take an actual driving test to get your license. Driver's education was offered at Robert E. Lee. I was the only student in my driver's ed class. James "Slick" Ellis was my teacher. Students couldn't call him Slick to his face. His proper name was James, but everybody knew him as Slick.

I had fallen in love with Slick's wife, who taught typing at Horace Mann. She never felt threatened by my admiration. I did really look forward to typing. It was an uncomfortable surprise to find that my driver's ed teacher was the husband of the woman I had fallen for in junior high school.

Our car was furnished by Buck Turner Chevrolet. It was a '52 four-door sedan, with standard transmission. It didn't come with air conditioning; however, some cars, such as the '54 Nash Ambassador, did have air conditioning. Air conditioning was introduced as early as 1933 in some of the luxury cars, such as limos and Cadillacs. The '52 sedan was the first car I drove that had electric turn signals. That device replaced the necessity of hand signals (elbow bent with hand up for a right turn; arm straight out for a left turn) which had been mandatory.

Because I was the only student, I got to drive the whole class time. Mr. Ellis (I was careful not to call him Slick) sat beside me as we toured the town. One time, he even allowed me to drive back home to get something I had forgotten to bring to school.

I passed, with a 95, and was legal to drive the old '46 Chevy and the '54 Ford.

It was such a beautiful car! A sort of beige with red (just the right shade) around the windows. It was our first V-8. The transmission was standard, four on the stick. No a/c.

At some point—I can't remember exactly when—I felt that the Lord was tapping me for some kind of special service. I had been elected chaplin of our high school band. I planned to enter a denominational college after graduating from high school to pursue God's will for my life.

We were still very active members at Stewart Heights Church (although somewhat hypocritical with our TV in "The Boy's House"). James Johnson was in the same grade as me, and he also wanted to go to college. We arranged a trip to East Texas Baptist College (now East Texas Baptist University). The '54 Ford took us there. More about that later.

I got a summer job at Gether's Paint and Body Shop. I was not skilled, but I was happy for a chance to make some money. One day, I drove the Ford to the shop. Lee was a master with paint. He wanted to doll up the Ford. I agreed, without informing my parents. It would cost us nothing, so what's the harm? Lee matched the red, and painted the rear fenders and the strip between the grill and the hood. We now had a unique paint job. There was no other '54 Ford that looked just like ours. That would bite me not much later.

My folks let me take the car on a date. The condition was that I would also take Robyn and her date. What fun can you have with your sister in the back seat? I had assured Mother that we would come straight home after the event. I had a curfew so, why not drop Robyn and her date off and then take my girl on home (after some strategic delay)? I drove Robyn and her date home. At the stop sign at Park and Pruett, a car passed us going the other way. I thought nothing of it.

When I got home (in time to beat the curfew), Mother was up. . .with something to say. "Why didn't you come home with your sister? I recognized the car!" Couldn't deny it. That was the only car painted that way. My sin had found me out. The discipline was not as severe as when I lied about the teacher's work period.

Between my junior and senior year at Robert E. Lee, I suffered an attack of appendicitis. I had surgery, with a local anesthesia. I remember how strange it seemed to hear the surgical team talking football and fishing while cutting me open. I healed fine, but the doctor wouldn't let me march with the band for two more weeks. It was a touch from heaven.

I had met a girl named Linda Rae Prince. I didn't know, then, that she had a younger sister, Catherine, who would be in our band. Catherine had endured surgery on her right foot during the summer, making her unable to march yet.

Mr. Burkett was our band director. What a man! He instructed Catherine and me to stay in the band hall and practice our instruments until we were able to march with the rest of the band. I was a klutz. She was a queen. . .princess (closer to her last name, Prince). She was more to me than Slick Ellis's wife had been! Couldn't keep my eyes off her—or my mouth shut.

For two weeks, we made beautiful music together—her on her clarinet and me on my bass horn.

I couldn't stand the fact that she was dating someone else. I began making a nuisance of myself, catching her after her boyfriend had left her to go on to his class. My full intention was to shoot him out of the saddle.

I think she felt sorry for me. She agreed to go with me to the spring play. We would double-date with Linda Rae and Charles. Charles had a '54 Chevrolet. It was his parents', but impressive. We went to the play. My heart was pounding. Catherine allowed me to kiss her goodnight! Ecstasy abounded!

The spring play was in March. Catherine and I dated the remainder of the school year, and continued—blissfully on my part—through the summer.

I was working for Lee Gether again that summer. Lee and his wife had two children, a girl and a younger boy. All the family worked around the shop, including the kids.

Most of the equipment in that paint and body shop was operated by compressed air. The paint guns had a double-action trigger. Pull it to the first stop, and you got compressed air to blow off the surface you were preparing to paint. Pull to the second stop, and paint would spray.

During a lull, I was chasing Lee's boy around the shop. In the nature of fun, he grabbed what he thought was a paint gun and aimed a blast of compressed air at me. What he had taken as a paint gun was actually a sand blaster. When he pulled the trigger, a blast of sand shot into my left eye. He was horrified, as we all were. I was rushed across the street to an optometrist (conveniently located). After applying a local anesthetic, the doctor removed more than 50 particles of sand from the colored portion of my eye. I left there with an impressive-looking bandage over my eye. What sympathy and care I got from Catherine that evening!

I was never much of a dater. We seemed content to play miniature golf, go to church activities, and such. Was I cheap, or just—as earlier admitted—a klutz? It didn't matter because she loved me!

We unofficially committed to one another. The official ring would come later. For now, I was in bliss because she so cared for me.

When I graduated, Catherine rode with us to deliver me to East Texas Baptist College (ETBC). We exchanged pictures, and vowed to write each day. It was too hard to leave her. Mail came during chapel. We had assigned seats, but just as soon as we were dismissed, I would run down the hill from the chapel to our dorm to relish my letter from Catherine.

Catherine tried out for twirler going into her junior year. Making that line may have surprised everyone except Catherine. She had a quiet self-confidence that wasn't flaunted, but evidenced. I would hitchhike home every time I had the chance. Letters couldn't suffice for a personal presence.

I was tutored on hitchhiking protocol. Always dress nicely. Suits weren't necessary, but slacks and an appropriate shirt were essential. Take a small suitcase. On one side, tape the letters "H-O-U-S-T-O-N" (one-inch adhesive worked well). Although I would get off before Houston, it was a well-known destination. On the other side, tape "E-T-B-C." We assumed that most would recognize those letters as some college.

Usually, you could get a ride out to Highway 46, leading to Henderson. Standing there, with the suitcase declaring your desired destination, you would hold out your thumb with what you hoped were compelling eyes that would cause motorists to find you irresistible. Normally, I could get close enough to home to call in four or five hours.

Catherine always worried about me hitchhiking. I was worried that I hadn't seen her.

That summer, we made our unofficial commitment official. I was more thrilled than I have words to express when she agreed to become my wife. She had one more year of high school. We planned to marry in June, a month after her graduation.

It was a sacrifice for Catherine to keep her commitment to me during this, her senior year. She defeated the odds and was elected drum major of the Robert E. Lee band. As such, she was in the spotlight, and invited to numerous events. She never complained when she had to have some friend or brother escort her.

It was during Catherine's senior year at Lee and my sophomore year at ETBC that I got my own first car—a 1950 model Nash.

1950 Nash

I was now a student at ETBC. The school had provided me with a work program that would help defray the costs of my education. Hubert and I were given the assignment of maintaining the floors in the various buildings on campus. We scoured the floors, mopped, and applied fresh wax, which we buffed with a machine we soon learned how to dance with.

We had what passed for a locker room in the basement of the administration building. We kept work clothes in our locker to change into from our class clothes. We, I had to admit, seldom washed those work clothes. My shirt got to the place where you couldn't even put it on backwards. My jeans would stand up by themselves. I actually pulled the top off rotting socks. Nothing to be proud of, but beyond denial.

We would move all the desks to one side of the room, clean the vacant floor, and then move the desks back—carefully—in order to complete the entire room. During the time we had to wait for the floor to dry (so we could buff), we had time to sit and visit.

I hadn't met Hubert until we became partners on the floor job. Hubert was a big man. He was from Leary, Texas, and had been offered a scholarship to play football in college. He declined because he was committed to prepare his life to pastor churches. We became very close friends. I was honored that Hubert agreed to be a groomsman at our wedding.

Hubert was called as pastor of Lone Pine Baptist Church near DeKalb, Texas. As we visited, he shared with me that the West Bowie Baptist Church, also near DeKalb, was without a pastor. Was I interested? I jumped at the chance.

Since I didn't have a car, I rode with Hubert to his home to spend the night before being taken to West Bowie. I learned, from Hubert and his father, to use rubbing alcohol as shaving lotion.

I met Fred Duncan at West Bowie. The good people there issued me an invitation to come be their preacher. It was my first church as pastor.

Hubert provided me with transportation for some time, but it was obvious—now that I was a pastor—that I must have a car of my own. Daddy had done better than "quite well" as a car salesman. His reputation for honesty and integrity brought customers back, and they also referred him to others. Daddy surprised me with a 1950 Nash sedan.

They don't make Nash anymore. In some ways, it was a classic. That model looked much like an inverted bathtub. There were no sharp lines on it. The car was a deep green, with blackwall tires. It was powered by a flat-head, six-cylinder engine.

I didn't have good luck with that car. I must have been at fault somehow, but it got overheated and cracked the engine block. I felt that we pushed the car further than we ever drove it. Problem after problem.

Still, some very interesting things happened during this chapter of my life. The Nash did get me back and forth to West Bowie. The kind folks there would host me overnight on Saturdays so that I wouldn't have to drive 75 miles or so, one way to the church. I relished the country hospitality and cooking. I was more pious, now that I look back at it, than I deserved to be. I remember when I decided to take on the evil of dipping snuff. With brash boldness, I stated from the pulpit that snuff, in a snake's mouth, would kill it. I thought my point would be persuasive. Mr. Payne brought me back to earth when he said, within earshot, "Snuff may kill a snake, but it doesn't do us any harm does it?"

West Bowie's building was in a clearing just off the road—if you could call that red-rutted path a road. During the colder months, it was a haven for black wasps. They lined the ceiling like a sort of artistic border. The building was heated by a wood stove in the middle of the building. Someone, likely Mr. Walker, would come early and light the fire. By the time the song service was over (Mrs. Payne would play when she was there), the building would be cozy enough that the wasps would begin to stir. It was a challenge to be faithful to my delivery while seriously concerned about where those wasps might land. I was never stung, but I was never really at ease while they were zooming around.

ETBC was a basketball school. Our gym was more like a barn with basketball goals at either end. Whenever I wasn't waxing floors or going to class, I would be at the gym getting into a pick-up game of basketball. That included the last day of classes. I had my grades and hoped to get one more game in before going back home—which would be an abbreviated trip since I had to ready a place for my soon-to-be bride and me to live.

There was a game in progress. Mostly we played half-court, so we could have a game at both ends of the court, and it cut the running in half. I could only come in when another player came out, so the sides would be even. Frank was much taller than me. He was determined to drive to the basket and lay his shot in. I was determined that I could block him out, so I set my block. My block didn't match Frank's determination. As he attempted to go over me, his elbow caught me square in the mouth. Two of my front teeth clattered to the floor.

What was I going to do? In just a month, I was to marry my sweetheart. Would she marry a toothless runt who couldn't block a shot?

I took my teeth and showed Mickey, our coach, the damage. He didn't like what he saw. Someone volunteered to take me to a dentist. I guess I learned that God is even interested in helping with teeth. I didn't know Dr. Sibley. He had been experimenting with root canals, and I would be a subject in his study.

He explained that he would remove what was left of a nerve in the teeth, sanitize them, put them back in where they had come out, and wire them in place. "Would I be OK for my wedding?"

"No reason why not. All that will be different will be that strand of silver wire that is holding the teeth in."

"Let's do it then!" I replied.

Funny how some things just root in your mind. As he was deadening my mouth, he injected a syringe into the roof of my palate. The needle broke!

I was sweating. He was calm. "Hadn't had that happen in a while," is all he said as he reloaded for another try.

With my teeth back in, I was ready to get home and assure sweet Catherine that I would be OK for the wedding. I would not want to disturb plans we had been counting on for so long.

Catherine and I had set the date for our wedding: June 29, 1957. She would graduate. I would rent us an apartment in Marshall (I had to stay there because of our church). If my memory is anywhere near accurate, I drove the Nash home for her graduation. I think that was the time that Daddy arranged for me to get a more dependable car—the 1954 Ford two-door.

1954 Ford Two-Door Sedan

I wouldn't be home that summer. Catherine and I were to get married in June, and I was serving as pastor at West Bowie Baptist Church. I came home to celebrate Catherine's graduation (any excuse to see her) and to visit with family.

As expected, Catherine was anxious about my teeth. I don't think the wedding was ever in jeopardy, but we were both concerned about how it would be affected. She was mostly concerned about my well-being. Had I suffered much with that accident? Was I sure that I was OK now? She was wrapped with concern for others, and I had the fortune of being somewhat special to her.

I could go back to Marshall with an easy heart. That easy heart had more than Catherine to thank. Daddy realized my concern about reliable transportation. The Nash had failed miserably. Since I was getting married and had that drive to West Bowie each weekend, he wanted me to have a better car—one that I could actually drive rather than push from place to place.

The Nash was replaced with a 1954 (newer model) Ford two-door sedan. It was a grey four-cylinder with a standard transmission. No a/c. It had a strange kind of after-market radio that fit OK in the dash, but had a funny-looking tuner. We expected that, since it was a four-cylinder—with a standard transmission, I would get very good gas mileage with it. Somehow, our expectations were without merit. We never got better than 14 miles per gallon. Our best figuring was that the rear-end was geared more for towing and that gearing reduced our gas mileage.

We would deal with that later.

After a sweet time (bittersweet, because I had to leave Catherine), I drove that Ford back to the apartment I had rented for us. I'd found us an upstairs furnished apartment. It was a duplex. Mrs. Duncan was our landlady. The bottom apartment was rented by students at ETBC, so we had good neighbors.

I got a job with East Texas Creameries. It was a local operation that made really good ice cream. Getting married, I needed some income. The job paid minimum wage (one dollar per hour). The manager whispered to me that, since I was getting married, he would see that I actually got $1.10 per hour.

There were four of us on the crew. I soon learned to disassemble the freezer and wash all the components for the next day's operation. I pulled popsicles from the brine tank. I learned how to make ice cream sandwiches. When we had over-runs or outdated products, we could take them home.

One of the tastiest tasks was catching the fudgesicle mix off the cooling tower into 40-gallon cans. The mix was sweet, chocolate, and sumptuous. As the mix would come off the tower, you could catch a cupful without disturbing the run. Yummy!

Hubert was also getting married that summer. Like me, he had already rented the apartment they would occupy. I invited Hubert to our place for supper. With some practice, I had perfected a menu of Spam®, potatoes, and green beans. I would slice off the amount of meat I wanted to fry (leaving the rest in the can and in the fridge). Frying the meat would leave me just the right amount of grease to fry my potatoes in. I would heat the green beans in a separate pot (this was well before the days of microwaves). Hubert was impressed and invited me to his place for a meal.

Hubert fixed the exact same menu that I had eaten with him. . .exactly! Spam® (remainder in the can in the fridge), potatoes, and green beans. We ate well enough to stay alive until we got a real cook in the place.

Our wedding was set for June 29, 1957. I arranged for time off and got permission to miss from West Bowie, and I went to Baytown to do what I could to assist in the ceremony.

Catherine was an exceptional seamstress. She had made several dresses—even designing some of them. She was determined to make her own wedding dress, which she did!

We did most of the decoration at First Baptist Church, Highlands, where we were married. We found yards of English Ivy on the grounds of the San Jacinto Monument. Mother took care of the rehearsal dinner. We each had six attendants, so it was quite a meal. One of Mother's specialties was cherry pie, and we had plenty at that meal. The reception was at Catherine's house in Highlands.

That house was a landmark in Highlands. Her Dad was in the lumber business. For a time, he had actually cut timber and processed it for sale in his lumber yard. He designed the house and built it with materials he had processed in his lumber yard. It was a two-story with four imposing pillars calling attention to the front of the house. The house was an appropriate white with a side-entry garage and a screened-in porch on the other side from the garage. You could never come into the kitchen without finding something delicious on the stove.

Both the Princes and the Craigs had large families. Brothers and sisters were included in the wedding ceremony. Brother Barnes officiated.

We decided to go to Galveston for our honeymoon. We had reservations at the Hotel Galvez, right on the seawall. Ray, Catherine's dad, allowed us to take his 1956 Oldsmobile on the honeymoon. That car could make you drool. It was a two-door hardtop, painted red and white (artistically applied). The whitewall tires were complimented with spinner hubcaps. We felt quite special driving off in that Olds.

I remember Daddy slipping me a 20-dollar bill just as we were leaving. One of Mother's brothers had given Daddy two dollars to pay the preacher that officiated at their wedding.

We drove to our reservation in Galveston. The car was parked in an open lot, and it was late June. When we got in it to take the ferry across to visit the church where one of my college friends was pastor, we were overwhelmed by stench. Well-wishing pranksters had put bait shrimp in the hubcaps. The sun had baked the shrimp to a distinctive stink.

Our pastor friend helped us find a place to get rid of the shrimp and to wash off the well-wishing signs painted with shoe polish on the windows.

We came back to Highlands to get Catherine's things that we needed to take back to Marshall.

Mrs. Duncan was very careful about her apartments. Catherine enrolled at ETBC where I was starting my junior year. We noticed that, when we returned from classes, Mrs. Duncan had been up checking to see that we were not trashing her apartment. We always locked the door, but she had her own key. We got past any resentment. Mrs. Duncan helped in our adjustment as she would regularly leave us a portion of those incredible pound cakes she made so well. We came to expect a wedge of cake on the stove when we returned from class.

I was thrilled to introduce Catherine to the folks at West Bowie. They were quite amazed that a sweet girl like Catherine would link up with a klutz like me. Mrs. Payne was not all that regular as our pianist. Catherine had taken a few piano lessons, but didn't consider herself a pianist. However, Catherine had such an obliging heart that when the people asked her to play, she would consent. She was most comfortable with songs that were in the key of C—no sharps and/or flats. We sang "Trust and Obey" and "Come Thou Fount of Every Blessing." Those songs became more than precious to us as age and illness invaded our lives.

We spent some of the weekend nights with the Duncans (no relationship to our landlady). Mrs. Duncan made world-class biscuits. I can still taste them, enhanced with just the right amount of butter and pear preserves. Catherine was as impressed as I was with those biscuits. "Could you show me how to make those biscuits," Catherine asked. The reply was, "I don't have any recipe, but you are welcome in my kitchen as I bake them." Catherine found you couldn't duplicate what Mrs. Duncan did. Mrs. Duncan went from canister to canister, a pinch of this, a handful of that, until perfect—beyond perfect—biscuits resulted. No one has ever been able to exactly duplicate Mrs. Duncan's biscuits.

We were assigned seats for chapel at ETBC. I sat toward the back with the upper classmen. Since she was a freshman, Catherine had to sit very near the front. I don't have words to explain how attractive she was. I do know that one of the boys who sat near her in chapel asked her for a date. She quickly and proudly showed her rings, embarrassing him but complimenting me on my bliss of having such a wife.

We had some exhausting times driving back and forth from the church and our parents' homes. We would be so sleepy that one would drive while the other fell into slumber. Many times, we would have to change every 30 minutes or so.

I had become involved with the Grange Hall Baptist Church, just out of Marshall. Our pastor was still a student at ETBC. Church had changed my life. I had made my profession of faith at the Stewart Heights Baptist Church in Baytown when I was in the sixth grade at Cedar Bayou Elementary. Stewart Heights was a very good church. They were very supportive and encouraging, but very conservative (no movies, no dancing, etc.). Much emphasis was placed upon the Second Coming of Christ. I wanted to be sure I was ready. Maybe as a result of my youth and that emphasis, I was plagued with doubts. I would dream that Jesus had come and I was not ready to go with Him. I hid my doubts, but was haunted by them.

Shortly after we married, Grange Hall sponsored a tent revival in Marshall. I can't remember the preacher's name, but I do remember coming down out of the choir to confess to him my doubts about my relationship with Christ. He suggested that I pray as if I had never entered into relationship with Christ. I did pray. I came away from that experience with an answer to my doubts.

I was baptized again. In looking back, I don't have complete answers. I think that experience was a step in my spiritual maturing. Was I already a Christian? I think probably so. I was, I know, seriously lacking in the assurance that would bring peace to my being. I think about that reference in Romans 5:10, "*. . .we shall be saved by His life.*" That experience, as I take it, was yet another step in my complete salvation. In a sense, every day I become more "saved." Does that make sense?

I was still trying to grow up. Not just in emotional maturity, but in spiritual maturity as well. In my haste (which God managed for my betterment), I withdrew us from ETBC. I fully intended to enroll in a very radical college in Tennessee. Parents attempted to influence, but I was too hard-headed.

We became members of First Baptist Church, Highlands. Jimmy Ponder was the pastor and the influence that God used to redirect—to correct—my intentions. Brother Ponder gave me opportunity to preach at the church. He arranged for me to meet with Dr. Guy Newman, who was president at Howard Payne College, Brownwood, Texas.

While we were deciding what to do, I had been able to get a job with General Telephone in Baytown. In those days, pay phones were popular. My job was to drive a company car to the various pay stations and collect the coins. I would empty the boxes into a canvas bag, tie it securely, and attach a note identifying the pay station. When I returned from my route, I would count the change with a remarkable machine that would count the quarters, dimes, and nickels. It was an amazing machine.

Daddy and I were trying to decide what to do about that poor gas mileage I was getting on that Ford. Another car might be the best answer, and I settled on a 1954 Oldsmobile. That car introduced us into the next chapter of living.

1954 Oldsmobile

Daddy and I were frustrated that my little Ford two-door got such poor gas mileage. It was, after all, a four-cylinder, with a standard transmission. By now, Daddy was doing well on his own. He had rented some space up on Highway 146, which was a major traffic artery through town. Someone painted him a sign, "Hiway Motors," and he did business on the strength of his integrity. Daddy carried the notes on most of the cars he sold. His honesty was rewarded by prompt payments most of the time. Car dealers in town would give Daddy a bid on their trade-ins—so he had a fairly wide inventory.

Included in that inventory was a nice-looking 1954 Oldsmobile. It was a two-door sedan in two-toned green. It was our first car with an automatic transmission. It was peppy, like Oldsmobiles have a reputation for. It did not have air conditioning.

By now, we were living in Highlands. For a time (until we wore out our welcome), we stayed with Catherine's grandparents. I had a job with General Telephone. Catherine would visit with Big Momma (her paternal grandmother) or walk across Main street to the house she grew up in.

The brakes needed replacing. I have fancied myself as a capable person, but without intelligent judgment about where to draw the limit on what I attempt to do. I would replace the brakes. I thought by doing the work myself, I would save some money. That was my intention.

While removing the spring that held the brake shoes in place, I clobbered myself between the eyes with the tongue-and-groove pliers I was using to remove the spring. You probably know that there is a proper tool for safely removing that particular spring. Since that accident, I have secured that tool.

The hit in the head produced a wound that required stitches. . .and cost me a day's work. So much for money saved!

As mentioned earlier, Brother Ponder arranged for me to meet Dr. Newman at Howard Payne. We set out early on a summer day in July. The route to Highway 290 was much simpler than today. We actually drove on "Jackrabbit Road," which has become that adventuresome Highway 1960. We had no credit cards; they weren't commonly available back then. I felt I had sufficient cash to make the trip.

I badly underestimated most aspects of this trip. Brownwood was much further than I guessed. The car got much less gas mileage than I expected (how had I complained about that little Ford?). It was hotter that we could get any relief from. What really threw me was the oil consumption of that Olds. It seemed that I spent more money for oil than for gas!

"Eternity" came to be defined by the duration of that trip. Would we never get there? Finally, well after dark, we came to a motel at the intersection of Highways 183/84 and 67. It was not a 3-star motel, but we were exhausted. It did have a shower and was air-conditioned. It seemed like the oasis we were desperate for.

We drove on from Early to Brownwood the next morning. In the daylight, we saw several newer motels on Highway 67 as we entered Brownwood.

The meeting with Dr. Newman went well. They agreed to help us with married student housing, and to give me some campus work to help with educational expenses.

The drive back to Highlands to complete our move to Brownwood was another adventure. The oil just kept burning out (we later found that a broken ring on one cylinder was letting the oil blow by). Just outside Cypress, I ran out of gas. Worse, I was out of cash! I walked back to a gas station and explained my dilemma.

Catherine was pregnant. We were exhausted. What could he do to help us. . .strangers that we were? Well, he gave me a five-gallon can of gas, with my assurance that I would stop on my way back to Brownwood and return his can and pay for that gas. God must have been helping us.

We announced to our folks our plans to move to Brownwood. It was a long way off. Catherine was beginning to show. I am still moved in my memory as I see her coming down the stairs with that maternity smock on. She was so huggable. In memory, she still is. As we were admiring her, she slipped—somehow—and made a good-sized bump on her shin. We were dressed for church. Big Daddy insisted on putting a dose of Absorbine Jr. on her leg. You may know what a medicinal odor that produced. . .and us on our way to church!

We knew we would have to make some arrangements for the coming of our first child. We insisted on moving together to the college (parents wanted us to delay or for Catherine to stay until after the baby came). Catherine did move with me, after we had assured our parents that the baby would be born with the care of our doctor in Baytown.

We had no furniture to move. The broken ring on the Olds had been repaired. We moved into what we came to know as the "Married Students' Apartments." There were six units in the complex. Each had a kitchen, a room that served as bedroom/den/dining room, and a bathroom. There was a pay phone between the stairs in the middle apartments. The walls were plaster, and the floors were finished concrete. We heated with natural gas. There was no air conditioning—fans had to suffice.

Howard Payne furnished our basic needs from surplus they had in one of their many storage facilities. In lieu of a double bed, we had two three-quarter beds that we crowded as close together as we could. An unfitted double sheet, placed crosswise, would cover both mattresses. We were afforded a table for dining and some accommodating chairs. There was a stove in the kitchen. Stark as it was, it was our first home—without parents and grand-parents—since Mrs. Duncan's apartment in Marshall.

We moved in between semesters. There was no one else living in our upstairs section of the complex. What memories I have of laying on that "super king-sized bed" with the windows wide open and the sweat beading from every pore. But, we weren't on the road, and we had each other.

Our doctor had estimated that the baby would come sometime in early August. We knew it was best to take Catherine back to her parents although she really would have preferred to stay in Brownwood, and I wanted that also. Despite the inconvenience of this essential separation, we drove back to Highlands. The plan was for her to have a safe delivery, and then I would bring her and the baby back to Brownwood. We packed her necessities and drove to her parents' house. It was sad for both of us when I had to drive away and leave her standing on the driveway blowing kisses.

I was surprised to get a call asking me to preach at a church in nearby Richland Springs. I jumped at the chance even though the Olds had sprung a leak in the fuel pump. Gas would spurt out the side of the pump. Bad gas mileage got worse. I was counting on some honoraria that would help pay for the extra gas that leaking pump was wasting. That pump caused me to miss a dessert of fresh peaches covered with homemade cream, a reluctant sacrifice.

I drove back down to see my precious wife. She was doing very well in her developing pregnancy. Catherine had taken very good care of herself. She was quite athletic from her discipline in twirling. It was sweet to be there. It was bitter to have to leave her there.

My folks thought it would be good for my brother, Randy, to go back to Brownwood with me. It was summer, and he was between years of high school and would be company for me as we waited for our first baby.

Daddy helped me exchange the Olds (I had replaced the pump. . .don't ask me to describe the details) for a 1946 Ford Sedan. It was exceptionally clean and should serve me well. Randy and I left Baytown to drive to Brownwood via Temple and Gatesville.

1946 Ford Sedan

This was a slick little sedan with a classic shape. It was black, powered by a flat-head V-8, with a standard transmission. My less than complete recall means that I can't remember whether it had a radio. I know it had no a/c.

After that difficult goodbye with Catherine, I drove over to Baytown and picked up Randy. Mother had fixed us some stuff to snack on while on the road. We left in early afternoon, planning to get into Brownwood before dark.

Our route was up Highway 36 to Gatesville, where we would connect with Highway 84 on into Brownwood. We were making good time up to the little town of Rogers. Just outside town, we threw a pully off the water pump on the left bank of cylinders. We couldn't go on, knowing that the engine would quickly overheat with that water pump disabled. We turned back to a shop we'd noticed when creeping through town where we'd had to strictly observe the speed limit signs. Rogers had a reputation for catching speeders. The shop would fix our problem if we could get the part. Temple, up the road some 11 miles, should have the part. We thought we could risk driving that far. Bad guess. Just barely out of town, we had to pull off the road.

It was around 3:00 in the afternoon. We thought it possible to catch a ride into Temple, get to a parts store before closing, and catch a ride back to Rogers. That was our plan. I am still not sure it was a good plan.

We locked the car and presented our thumbs to oncoming traffic. The first car that saw us stopped and let us ride with them into Temple. We had to walk to whatever parts store we could find. We did find a store—actually,

31

more than one. Each store either did not have the part for that old a car or was closing just as we walked up.

So, here we were, in Temple, with no part and no place to spend the night. Our only hope was to catch a ride back to the car, spend the remainder of the night there, and start over in the morning. We walked back to Highway 36 and started thumbing back toward Rogers. The good luck we had leaving Rogers was not our experience returning to Rogers. It was as though our thumbs were invisible. Cars whizzed by, totally unconcerned about our situation.

It was getting dark and with the encroaching darkness, it became less likely that we would get a ride. We had no option but to walk. We did walk, in dusk and deepening darkness. Just on the outskirts of Rogers (not more than a mile out) we were picked up by a carload of drinkers wondering if—since that area was "dry"—we knew where they could find some booze at that hour. We knew we were in trouble when beer bottles spilled out of the car when the door was opened to let us in.

We had walked at least 10 miles. We welcomed the uncomfortable accommodations of that little car. . .and fell into exhausted sleep.

In the morning cool, we risked driving back into Rogers to get the car fixed. A mechanic drove into town and got the part. How, though, were we going to pay that bill? We called Daddy. He agreed to stop in Rogers on a trip in that direction and pay the bill. The shop was willing to take my watch as security. We drove our repaired little car on to Brownwood. A week or so later, Daddy stopped in Rogers and redeemed my watch.

The plan was for Randy to keep me company while we waited for the baby. We didn't know then that the doctor had misread his signals. The baby would actually come more than a month after the date he had projected. Since we didn't know that yet, every ring on that pay phone stirred our hope.

Randy and I were just about to get up one morning when we heard that downstairs phone (remember, there was only that phone in the complex). Randy, being younger, beat me down the stairs. I heard the door slam behind him, and—momentarily—the phone stopped ringing. I waited anxiously. Was this that call we had been expecting? I heard Randy slowly coming back up the stairs. As soon as he opened the door, I pounced on him with my eager hope. "Who was that?" I asked.

"Someone wanted to know if we had Prince Albert in a can. If we did, we should let him out." I was disgusted. . .and disappointed.

My work on the campus of Howard Payne was different from my work at ETBC. I wasn't doing floors. I was mowing grass and moving furniture. We had a big (maybe 40-inch cut) walk-behind mower. It was too big to simply push. A clutch engaged and disengaged the power that propelled that mower.

Randy and I had just walked, two days before, more than 10 miles. Now, here was this mower that required following. John, my campus boss, was OK with Randy helping me mow. Help appreciated.

I had to get Randy back home for school, and I really wanted to see Catherine. We would trust that our little Ford would safely get us there. . .and it did.

Given the history we had endured getting parts and so forth, we agreed that a later model car would be wiser. Daddy had earned his own lot by this time and had a sturdy-looking 1952 Chevrolet two-door hardtop for which we could trade our Ford.

1952 Chevrolet Two-Door Hardtop

Since we had agreed that a more dependable car was advisable, Daddy showed me this neat-looking hardtop. The bottom of the two-tone was a lime green (it really looked as if it had been hand-painted with a brush). The top was black. Like our previous Oldsmobile, this car had an automatic transmission. Chevrolet called it, "Powerglide." It sounded much like a jet plane and gave the sound that made you think you were going faster than you were.

It appeared a more than satisfactory replacement for the Ford.

Leaving Randy at home and saying goodbye—again—to my sweet wife, I drove back to Brownwood. The apartment seemed to have become larger, since I was now alone.

I drove the hardtop back to Baytown on the date we had been told to expect delivery. When it didn't happen, I knew I would have to go back. Daddy insisted that I drive the family's car—that 1954 Ford station wagon with the custom paint—back, so that I would have something to make a hurried trip in when the baby was ready.

I went back to work on the campus, but I knew that we would need some cash. My work on campus, like at ETBC, was only applied to my bill at school. I learned that Wiseman's—a department store downtown—had an opening. At the time, the minimum wage was $1.00 per hour. Few employers in Brownwood paid minimum wage. With the large number of hungry students to draw from, pay was whatever that particular employer wished. I went to work at Wiseman's for 75 cents per hour. It wasn't much, but it was better than nothing and more than I was presently making.

I was the gofer. Whatever they needed, I would go for. I helped the display manager dress the windows. I took out trash. I swept floors. I got a paycheck.

One of the new persons I had met told me that Lamkin Brothers was hiring college students (one of the brothers was a trustee at Howard Payne) and that they paid minimum wage! I hurried out there as rapidly as my little hardtop would go. I got there in time to be hired.

When I went to inform Mr. Wiseman that I had found another job, he didn't take it well. . .at all! "OK," he said, "but you are the last of those college kids I am hiring." I didn't know whether to feel bad for any possible future job seeker or to be glad that they wouldn't have to work in such a hostile environment.

Lamkin's made feed blocks for livestock. Their plant was out on one of the railroad sidings at the old, abandoned Camp Bowie. The blocks were produced by dropping a measured amount of feed (usually 40 pounds) from a hopper (operated by an electric button) into the throat of a hydraulic press. These presses got their strength from large, loud electric motors next to each press.

The press had two levers. The lever on the left (as you faced the machine) dropped the die that had received the feed from the hopper. The lever on the right lowered the top plunger to tightly squeeze the feed into a block. Each press had a gauge that indicated when enough pressure had been reached. The operator would release the lever controlling the upper plunger and allow the bottom plunger to bring the freshly formed block up to the surface of the die.

The operator would pull the block from the die and place it on a table just to his back. There, a "wrapper" would wrap the block, taping the ends and slapping a label on the top of the completed block.

Carts were pulled behind the wrapper, and the wrapped blocks were stacked until the cart was loaded. The full cart was pulled (by a World War II surplus tug) to either a waiting truck or to a designated place in the warehouse.

Each crew had three people mixing the feed and teams of two for each press. Usually, one of the mixers would drive the loaded cart to wherever it was needed.

I worked the shift from 4:00 in the evening until 11:00.

It was very dirty work. The dust was constant. . .everywhere. When mixing (we often traded around on tasks), we used a lot of iron oxide, which we knew as red iron. Red iron may as well have been a dye. Nothing would take it out. The best washing could do was tone it to a more pleasant pink.

Our baby was not late, but we were still waiting. The doctor, as earlier noted, had missed the expected date. Catherine and I talked (that solitary pay phone). She wanted to come on to Brownwood. We could have the baby here. We agreed that, although it was painful, it was better for her to stay there until the baby came.

Just before shift change one evening, I got a call on Lamkin's shop phone. It was Catherine. In a calm voice (she was trying to keep me from urgency), she informed me that she was on the way to the hospital. "Might not be anything, but we think it is best that we go." How I agreed.

I told the crew chief that I had to go. I rushed home and bathed (that red iron was too much to carry back to meet our first child). The trip would consume near six hours. I hit a railroad crossing too fast, and the muffler and tail pipe fell off on the road. It was good that I had that station wagon, as I had to carry the muffler and tail pipe with me. The rest of the trip was a little louder.

I got to Baytown Hospital around 5:00 a.m. The baby had come. She was the most beautiful little girl in the nursery—and that was not just my opinion. My first impression was how daintily she folded her beautiful little graceful hands under the chin of that precious face. She was born on September 26, 1958. How could a klutz like me now have two beautiful girls?

When we got the OK to leave the hospital, we made plans to take our new little family to Brownwood, our home.

We had been able to move into one of the downstairs units. Since school had started, two new couples had moved in our complex. We became close friends with Dale and Lou Cain and Haskell and Elaine Wilson. The Wilsons lived in the unit that had been our first address there. The Cains lived across the hall—the best description I have for that little landing between the doors of those apartments.

We still had some of that furniture the school had scrounged up for us. We had been given a double bed and had some fitted sheets that would make sleeping more like what it ought to be. When I brought that bed home, the first thing I did—although tired from the drive—was set it up and put on those fitted sheets.

Everyone we had met shared our joy over the arrival of our beautiful Cheryl Kay. She was healthy with a vigorous appetite. She was gaining weight at an encouraging rate. However, about the time that she was approaching six weeks, we began to notice that although she would eat well, she would vomit most of it back up. We were alarmed, and made an appointment with Dr. Rogers Coleman at the Medical Arts Hospital in Brownwood.

We were young. We were new in town. We were new parents. The doctor asked about Cheryl's vomiting. "Does she just spit up, or is it more like a volcano spewing out?" It was the latter. Dr. Coleman advised us to admit her into the hospital (which was a serious move for us as first-time parents). Examinations revealed that she had pyloric stenosis. We had to have that explained.

In lay terms, the pyloric valve connects the stomach with the small intestine. For some reason, this valve was not functioning properly. Since the food couldn't digest, it would sour in her little stomach producing that violent vomit. There was a procedure that had proven to correct this malfunction. For some reason, a pie-shaped wedge could be surgically removed from that valve and solve the problem.

We had to submit our baby to surgery. Dr. Justice would be the surgeon. Dr. Coleman would continue as our attending physician.

We were assured that the surgery went well. Then, we had to wait for evidence that food would pass through this modified valve. Cheryl was dependent upon liquids supplied through IVs for sustenance. She was too little to offer large enough veins to accommodate the necessary needles. For the first few days, needles were inserted into the muscles of her little thighs. Her hands were tied to the bed to keep her from pulling at the IVs. She had to lay on her back. All she could have to satisfy her sucking function was a nipple stuffed with cotton and wet with sugar-water.

We anxiously awaited evidence that the modified valve was working. Time crept by. She was suffering, and we felt so helpless. As we waited, the IVs in her little legs became inadequate. They were able to find a large vein in her little head, and began fluid there. We waited and prayed. She needed a unit of blood. Peggy and Herman lived in the last apartment before the street. They had a daughter, Kim. They were among our precious friends. Peggy volunteered to give blood, but we still had no evidence that anything was getting through that valve.

Catherine's parents called. They asked about contacting the doctor they had used, in Houston, when their babies needed attention. We talked with Dr. Coleman about it. Dr. Qualtrow suggested trying a very thick rice cereal. The hope was that the thick mixture would stay in her stomach and resist any throwing up.

We had never been so happy with a dirty diaper! The thickened cereal did the trick! Our little girl has grown up to be a model mother and grandmother. We rejoiced in the blessing of her healing and of her precious life.

I had been given the opportunity of pastoring a half-time church (met every other week) in Energy, Texas, about six miles off Highway 36 between Comanche and Hamilton. The folks there were farmers, dairymen (and women), and ranchers. There was the church building and a general store that also served as the post office. Coda and her son, Jay Lee, ran the store.

That store was an experience. The walls were lined with cane-bottom and rope-bottom chairs. There was a chest-type soda-water cooler in one corner of the store. The post office occupied another corner. Protocol was to check the mail, buy whatever groceries were needed, get a drink out of the cooler, and sit in one of the chairs and visit. The store was like a big family room.

The folks took us in as if we had always been there. Most of the people were close to the ages of our parents. Some still had children or grandchildren in the school in Gustine (they played six-man football at Gustine). We quickly learned the protocol at Energy. After church on Sunday evenings, the congregation would gather at the store to drink from the cooler and visit. Cheryl learned to drink from a straw while sitting on Gayle's lap. Her drink of preference was orange.

I was still working at Lamkin Brothers, so we had some consistent income—not much, but income went further in those days. With the commute to Energy, I felt we needed a better car than this reliable '52 Hardtop.

Bob Armstrong was paying for his education by selling used cars at the local Ford dealership. He recognized my need. . .and that a sale could address his need also. We made a deal to trade my '52 Hardtop for a '54 Bel Air.

1954 Chevrolet Bel Air

It was a two-door with an automatic transmission—Chevrolet had vastly improved their old Powerglide. It had a classy paint job—a sort of butterscotch brown on the bottom, with cream on the top. Besides my folks' Ford station wagon, this was the best-looking car we'd had (I can't include that '56 Olds 98 that we took on the honeymoon).

I was a little nervous about driving it when it was my turn to carpool the crew to Lamkin's. What would that red iron do to my upholstery? We felt very comfortable driving to Energy.

For some reason, our car did not come equipped with a deluxe heating system. Rather than having a switch on the dash that would allow changing the airflow from your feet to defrost, you had to reach down to the air-handler and manually change the vents to defrost.

In those days, babies were permitted in the front seat. We had little Cheryl in her seat between us. It was cold this Sunday morning, and the windshield was beginning to fog up. As we were approaching a bridge over one of the creeks under Highway 36, I attempted to change the airflow. As I reached across the seats, I was not aware that I had pulled the car slightly to the right. . .the direction in which I was reaching. We collided with the bridge railing. Thankfully, there was no oncoming traffic. We jerked to a stop, with the only apparent injury a scrape on Catherine's back from Cheryl's car seat.

It was snowing slightly. We were fortunate to have a passing motorist stop and agree to take us on to Energy. The folks had gathered for church and wondered why we weren't there yet. We all teared and cheered together that we had survived the accident, but I still deal with some guilt about my part in causing it.

After church, Jack drove us back to Brownwood.

Our chapter with this Bel Air was too short. The car was totaled. The collision had ruined the rear-end, and repair/replacement was greater than the value of the car. Insurance helped us get a 1953 Chevrolet from Bob Armstrong.

1953 Chevrolet Two-Door

They didn't have an exact match for the car I had wrecked. They did have a very stout '53 Chevrolet, a step down in class from the Bel Air I had ruined. This car was painted a sort of generic blue (maybe General Motors patent?). I remember it having blackwall tires with bottle-cap hubcaps. It did, in contrast to our last one, have a heater that could be controlled from the dash.

We accepted the car, and thus began this next saga.

I was being deeply influenced by the Bible courses I was taking. I had opted to major in Bible, with a minor in history. My first class was taught by Dr. Tracy. From that experience, I scheduled as many classes as I could with him. Dr. Tracy stretched your brain. I can see him comfortably seated behind a plain desk. He would rest his elbows on the desk and roll a pencil between his palms as he aggravated us with probing questions.

I was coming from a very fundamentalist background. When Dr. Tracy first said, "Love yourself properly," I was ready to write him off as too liberal. I hadn't been so challenged to think. It was enough to do as instructed. Dr. Tracy expected us to think.

An example of his process was a paper he required. He instructed us to write a paper on "Righteousness by Faith" and to do so in 25 words of less! To our complaints, he explained that if we learned to compress our thoughts, we could expand them as needed. Challenged.

Another half-time church, Wilson, contacted me about coming to preach for them. Both churches, Energy and Wilson, were in the same general direction. . .off Highway 36 between Comanche and Hamilton. Energy was to the right, Wilson to the left. We were excited about the opportunity. On the Sundays when we weren't at Energy or Wilson, we attended Calvary Church in Brownwood.

The Wilson church met in an old school building that was no longer being used. The congregation was small, but they took us in as family. We got one of our favorite recipes from Mrs. Turner while there. Her okra and tomatoes couldn't be beat.

Cotton Wilson (not sure if any kin to whomever they named that community for) and his family were regular members of the church. They lived on a hill (we would, in that setting, call it a mountain) that was surrounded by a creek and woods. In bad weather, it was not unusual to see them come to church on a tractor. It was the only way they could get in or out.

One Sunday morning, Cotton asked if we liked chicken. He certainly already knew the answer to that! "Sure," I replied. He would bring a couple of fryers to church that night. I am not sure what we were expecting, but he brought us two live chickens bound together at the feet. We left them tied until after class Monday morning. There was a little yard space between our apartment and the portable buildings that had been brought in for needed classroom space. We had our clothesline in that small space.

I took the chickens, fully alive, to prepare them for the stove. I had seen country folks place a mop handle over the chicken's neck and pull the head off by jerking the legs. That was how I executed those chickens. I overheard one of the kids as she was going into class say, "He just pulled its head off." I expect that may have been the first time she had seen such an operation.

As in most of the early churches we served, different families would have us for the afternoon between morning and evening services. If there were visits to be made, we would be informed as we ate and fellowshipped with our host family.

This Sunday, we followed Cotton Wilson home. It was an isolated homesite. Catherine was helping Mrs. Wilson with the after-dinner dishes. If you knew Catherine, you would know how sweet and gentle she was. In her kindest voice, as she was drying dishes, she asked Mrs. Wilson about using the restroom. "Just go outside and shut your eyes," was the response she got! The place was isolated, but to that extent?

I was still working at Lamkin's, so I either had to go to work at 11:00 p.m. on Sunday or 3:00 a.m. on Monday.

With my minor in history, I was in several classes with Mr. Preston. He was as into history as if he had lived it. Mr. Preston dictated every note we took. He was our text. I laugh as I review some of those old notes. . .to see how my fatigue affected my writing. On many pages, the pen would default from writing to slipping to the edge of the page, where the bump would wake me back up. I also saw an occasional drool-drop where I surrendered to sleep.

The grandparents were anxious to see our sweet Cheryl, so we made a quick trip down there. The agreement was that the Princes would bring her back home in a week or so.

On the way back to Brownwood, just outside Lampasas, the windshield wipers suddenly flipped across (it was not raining), and the car died. We caught a ride into town and arranged for a wrecker to pull our car in. We took a bus on to Brownwood. I would call to see the damage. It turned out that we had broken the timing chain. It could be replaced. It would have to be repaired.

I bussed back to Lampasas to pick up the car. I wondered if I could continue to trust it. We continued to drive the '53 to work, to the two churches, and wherever—always with a degree of doubt.

The 1954 Mercurys had a style that caught my eye. I had no real reason, other than wanton desire, to consider trading in order to get one. That sad episode will be discussed in this next chapter.

1954 Mercury

If I would have let common sense rule, I would not even be writing this chapter. There was nothing wrong with our '53 Chevrolet. The fix on the timing chain put us in good stead with it. However, I could not satisfy my craving until I got into one of these classy-looking Mercurys.

I started shopping around the used car lots in Brownwood. I spotted a sweet gray one at a lot on Highway 67 coming into town. I suffocated common sense, and began a conversation with the salesman. I drove the car. That was a mistake. I couldn't control my out-of-control appetite. He tried to help me back to sanity by quoting a deal that was too much for me to handle. Catherine was tolerant of my addiction with cars and drove whatever I came home with.

I spotted another '54 Merc at yet another lot—I was like a drunk, looking for a bar that would allow me credit! I should have driven away. When I got in to start the car, the key wouldn't work in the ignition. The salesman knew the trick, and he got it to work for me. We drove it, and he sensed my addiction and made a deal that I should have resisted. . .but didn't.

Now, we were paying for a 1954 green Mercury (with a tricky ignition). It did look nice, and my addiction was sated for a time. My contentment was to be very short-lived. As I was driving my turn in the car pool, the Mercury suddenly screeched to a halt. The rear-end had completely locked up.

One of the crew called his wife (they were sensible, and had a car they could afford), and they took us on to work. My Mercury was towed to the shop.

The Ford/Mercury shop told me what damage to expect if I opted to fix the car. This was the same dealership where my old car-trading friend, Bob, worked. He helped me work a deal. I was determined, this time, to get a car that would stand up to our schedule—if I could afford one. We came to terms on a 1957 Ford Fairlane 500.

1957 Ford Fairlane 500

I justified the purchase of this very nice car on the basis of the drive we had to make to our new church at Agee. I did have to justify my thinking to more sensible companions that felt I had gotten too fancy.

The Fairlane was a two-door sedan. The color scheme was a very nice green and green. One of the greens was a sort of avocado. The chrome lines were artistic. Tires were whitewalls. The transmission was a standard on the column, with overdrive. Overdrive kicked-in when you reached a determined speed, and the transmission would shift into a higher gear. Gas mileage was supposed to be better than my previous car.

Folks from Agee had come over to Energy to hear me preach. They invited us to come audition for them (we say they "extended a call"). Agee was a pretty farming community between Hamilton and Meridian. The closest town was Cransfills Gap. There was a little cemetery beside the Methodist church just as you turned off the main road. The Baptist church was about four miles up the road, just approaching a 90-degree curve. It was an inviting white building with a steeple. Beside the building was the brush arbor where summer revivals were held.

The folks there liked us, and asked us to come preach for them. We had grown to love the people at both Energy and Wilson, and were sad to have to leave. They understood, and we moved from being the pastor of two half-time churches to a church that met every Sunday.

I was also foreman on the graveyard shift at Lamkin's. That meant that I had to be at work Sunday night at 11:00. Catherine was not only a good wife, she was a good driver. We had learned early on to swap out when one got too tired to drive safely. She would drive home on Sunday evenings as I attempted to sleep.

Coming home out of Hamilton, Highway 36 has some steep and curving hills to navigate. Some of the hills are so steep that passing lanes have been built to allow slower trucks (slowed because of their loads) to pull over so that normal traffic can continue. As we were coming down from the crest of one of these steep hills, Catherine woke me up saying, "Look here, Bob." There were two trucks attempting to pass as they climbed the hill! There was no passing lane on our side. The oncoming trucks took up the entire highway. We prayed as she turned the car into the gravelly shoulder. Our car began to skid. It was one of those moments when time seems slowed. Almost as if we were outside the experience, we felt an uncommon calm. Without panic, I heard myself say, "Just turn the wheel in the direction of the skid, honey." She did, and we did a 360 on that shoulder, backing to a rest in the shallow ditch along the road.

The trucks never slowed. We watched as their taillights disappeared over the crest. Now, safe and stopped, our emotions reacted. We hugged one another. There were some tears. Our sweet baby Cheryl never woke up in the back seat. I drove the rest of the way home.

It was during this chapter that a couple of memorable things happened at Lamkin's. We had gone from cottonseed meal in 100-pound bags to cottonseed in bulk. All our mixes used a lot of cottonseed meal. In fact, it was the main ingredient in most of them.

A huge bin was installed in the warehouse where all the feed components were stored. A portable bin was provided that allowed us to push it under the large bin, open a gate, and fill our little bin with however much meal the formula called for.

Very often, the cottonseed meal would hang up and refuse to fall out. A nice rubber hammer had been provided with which to pound on the side of the storage bin until the meal would break loose. Walter was helping me mix one evening. He rolled the bin over beneath the cottonseed meal storage. When he slid open the gate, nothing happened. He banged tenderly on the side of the bin. Nothing. He banged with a little more intensity.

Still nothing. Then, Walter put his whole heart into that hammer. Bam, bam, bam. Then, with a resounding "whoosh" the whole load of meal came rushing down through that open gate. Walter disappeared in a cloud of cottonseed meal dust. In a moment, he came staggering out—pushing that over-loaded portable bin—with only the blue of his eyes showing through that dirty brown of cottonseed meal dust.

Seems that Walter and I had more adventures. He was always ready to help, and I seemed to always need some help.

Most of our components came by rail, many in boxcars. Lamkin's had an old Diamond-T truck that was used to move the cars to the doors where a ramp was placed between the opened door of the boxcar and the warehouse. We would use hand trucks to off-load the materials. Very often, we would be asked—on our late shift—to off-load these cars.

A switch engine would pull the loaded cars to our siding, leaving the first one that we were to off-load at the door of the warehouse. The other cars would be ahead, where they could be pushed down (with that Diamond-T) to the door. The empty car would be pushed out of the way by the latest car. One of the crew would ride the empty car to set the brake when the car had cleared. The brakes on the cars were activated by a wheel on the front of the car. Turning the wheel tightened the brakes. Several turns were required to effect a stop. Most cars were so heavy that they didn't move easily. Setting the brakes nearly always was accompanied by a slight bump into the last car pushed there.

I was driving the Diamond-T. Walter was riding the brake. As usual, we heard a slight bump as our car bumped into the one we had just finished off-loading. We made a joke about how funny it would be if that car just kept rolling. Walter climbed down to see—the car was gone! The bump had sent it rolling down the track!

We hoped we could retrieve that offending car before the day crew came on. We found a coil of really big rope—about one inch in diameter. The plan was to take the Diamond-T down the track until we found our car. Surely that big rope would be strong enough to pull a car that rolled that easily back "home."

We found the car. It was a good quarter of a mile down the track. The grade steepened down, so the car had to be going pretty fast when it passed the open door of another plant on the siding. Just past that open door, the track ended with a strong barricade. Our car had bounced off that barricade until it finally came to rest.

I had to back the truck down the track to where our vagrant car was resting. There was a gentle curve in the railbed, but we navigated it OK. Eventually, we backed close enough so Walter could attach our giant rope. With us tethered together, I put the T into low-low and began a noisy crawl back up the track.

The hum of the lowest gear drowned out any other sound. It was a clear night, with a full moon. It seemed our plan would succeed. We would get the boxcar back before anyone knew of our blunder. I don't know why I happened to look in the side-view mirror, but I did. I saw Walter, running as fast as he could across those ties and waving his hands frantically.

I stopped the truck to see what Walter's concern was. The car was not following me. "When did the rope break?" I asked.

"Just as soon as you put some tension on it," said Walter.

We limped back to the mill. The switch engine came before the day bosses and went down to retrieve our car. We felt saved. What an adventure!

It was during this time that we learned that we were going to have another baby. I think it was because she had taken such good care of herself, that Catherine fared so well in her pregnancies. We used Dr. Coleman. He had been so special to us since that ordeal with Cheryl. We expected the baby sometime in June, maybe mid-June. The expected time came and went. We even tried inducing (Catherine was such a game sport to endure such). Nothing, yet. We were riding the swing set at a park when Catherine's waters broke.

We rushed to Brownwood Hospital; the Medical Arts Hospital in Brownwood had closed by then. Christi Gayle became the only baby in the maternity ward July 7, 1960.

She was more than worth the wait. From the very first day, she had—and exercised—her own mind. We were concerned that she might have some problems. She had none.

Christi had to sleep in the basinet. Cheryl was very comfortable in her crib. We were a blessed and happy family.

Cheryl had regained the weight she had lost due to her surgery and recovery. Since she had to go for so long without a bottle, she really loved when she could cuddle up with her bottle and suck down the nourishment. When she would finish with her bottle, she would take it by the nipple and flip it over the bed. The bottle didn't fare well on those concrete floors. We were attempting to wean her off the bottle, but she loved it so much. Finally, after cleaning up broken bottle after broken bottle (collision with the floor), we told her that when she broke another bottle that was it. And, it was.

Christi fought sleeping. Catherine exhibited what must have been natural mothering skills. She would, without coaching, wrap Christi tightly—so that she couldn't flail her arms—and lay her on her side. After only a few moments of fussing, the baby would go to sleep. I didn't marvel as much then—at her mothering abilities—as I do now in reflection. She was much more than I fully appreciated at the time.

The Sunday after Christi's birth, Catherine needed to (had to) stay home with the baby. I took Cheryl with me to Agee. I didn't do that well at dressing her. Fixing her hair was my hardest task. Nettie took Cheryl to sit with her during church. She also made some order out of my disorder.

We bought our first clothes washer after Christi was born. We lived in that time before disposal diapers. With two girls in diapers, we were exhausting our budget and ourselves with trips to the local washateria. I think our first washer was a Frigidaire. It had wheels so we could roll it up to the kitchen sink and use a special adaptor to connect it to the water supply. We didn't have a dryer, so that line in the back was crowded with drying diapers.

The folks at Agee, like the people at Energy and Wilson, were great beyond description. They took us in as though we were family. Jake and Jewell Kinney were especially good with Cheryl. There was a minor scuffle each Sunday over who would have Cheryl during and after church. Jake treated Cheryl as his own granddaughter. One Sunday, we were having dinner with the Kinneys. Jake took Cheryl out to see the cows (they were in the dairy business). It was a clear and brisk day. The calves were frolicking about. Jake asked Cheryl if she would like to ride one. Her reply has become a part of Craig folklore, "No, he's too hunk!"

Jake and Jewell thought Cheryl needed a dog. We accepted the mutt they offered. I rigged a sort of fence in what was our backyard at the apartment complex. Cheryl named the pup, Ruff.

Cheryl used to sit on the steps of our apartment and greet the students as they walked by on their way to class. As mentioned earlier, behind and to the right of us were portable buildings that served as classrooms. One morning, Catherine came out to get Cheryl and couldn't find her! After frantically looking in all the apartments and around the general area, Catherine was relieved to see Cheryl coming out of one of those portables. She was struggling to snap the suspender on her overalls. She had gone into the building to use the restroom.

Chock Broyles used to sit in the pew behind Catherine. He would reach out to touch Christi, and say, "She's my chunk of gold." Chock had lost his wife, Mae, during a fog-invasion that made it impossible for me to drive back in time to conduct the funeral. As soon as I could, I went to visit with Chock. Theirs was a large house with a comforting front porch. We sat, and Chock began to talk. He told of how he and Mae used to sit and hold hands as they read the Bible. He was having an awful time adjusting to her death. "Bob," he said, "one night as I was grieving my loss, God showed me where Mae is. I am OK now." They are both in heaven now. What a reunion we will have in God's time!

The kids in the community went to school in Fairy, Texas. A boy named Don dated a girl named Peggy. Peggy's uncle was a Methodist preacher. Don's folks were farmers and ranchers. Don and Peggy were in the last class before Fairy School closed down. The friendship that began there has grown into a lasting relationship.

We held our summer revival under the tabernacle. The benches were handmade out of 2 x 4 pine slats. The pulpit sat on a platform. Lights were strung along the ceiling beams. At least once, we had an armadillo bump into the platform—challenging the attention of the congregation and the preacher.

I took a job with Swift and Company's feed mill and hatchery. My job was to work with Mr. Clausen who oversaw the hatchery. Swift supplied turkey poults for a host of growers who would take the poults and grow them to maturity. One of my tasks was to transfer the eggs into more advanced incubators used to complete the process. From time to time, we would find an egg that was not developing—it was merely cooking. These were called "exploders," and we would toss them into a 55-gallon trash barrel. They would land with a boom! Twice a week, we would the sort the poults into vented boxes for delivery to various growers. As in most native births, we had to deal with certain birth defects—extra legs, misshaped necks. The humane thing to do was to destroy these defective birds. I asked Mr. Clausen if I could have some of those that weren't beyond some patient care. He agreed, and I got into the deformed turkey business.

The married student housing complex was never fully occupied. I seized upon one of the vacant apartments as a place I could grow these turkeys (I had feasts in mind). I arranged some adequate housing for my birds, and began regular feeding.

My flock was growing. . .not only in size, but also in number. Everything seemed smooth and routine. I would check on the birds daily. They were growing well. I could almost taste turkey.

One ill-fated afternoon, Mr. Garvin, the financial officer at Howard Payne, came to show a prospective couple the married student housing. When he opened the door of my turkey farm, he was not pleased. After a rather harsh lecture, I had to vacate my farm.

Ed Russel was the pastor at Jones Chapel Baptist Church in Early, just east of Brownwood. I had met Ed in one of our classes. Jones Chapel was one of those churches a student-pastor dreams of. It was close to school. It provided a parsonage. I visited with Ed about my turkey farm. To my surprise, he told me that there was a chicken coop in the back of their house. He would be OK with me taking my turkeys there. We both tired of the feeding routine, and the turkeys grew to eating size. Most of them went to the Thanksgiving dinner at Jones Chapel. We had one, but the taste did not make up for the trouble.

By now, I was ready to graduate. My folks had come up for the ceremony. On the very day of the ceremony, we loaded what we had into a rented trailer, and moved to Ft. Worth. Our plans were for me to enter seminary. We had rented a little two-bedroom house in southeast Ft. Worth, not far from the seminary. We had no furniture except for our bed and the baby's crib (Chris was still in her basinet). We went into downtown Ft. Worth to buy a dinette set, a bed for Cheryl, a bedroom suit, and something for the family room.

Cheryl had shown that she was an adventuresome spirit. We had not even met our neighbors when we realized that Cheryl was missing. Panic is too gentle a word for the emotions that were flooding our minds. We quickly met the adjoining neighbors. No one had seen her. Desperation. As if out of the blue, Cheryl walked into our yard as if nothing was wrong. She had seen a vacant storage building and went in to explore. We felt relief and vowed renewed diligence to keep her in sight.

We knew I would have to find a job—one that would also allow me to attend seminary. At that time, Ft. Worth had a big contract with the defense department to produce aircraft. When we arrived in town, a big layoff (between contracts) was deflating the economy. It looked like a bad time to be looking for work.

I heard about a General Mills plant in Blue Mound, on the extreme north of Ft. Worth. They were hiring, but required shift work. I explained to Mr. Black, the plant manager, that I had come to Ft. Worth to continue my education. I had to have work, but asked that he be aware that when—and if—I found a job that would allow me to work and attend seminary, I would take it. He agreed, and I signed on.

The General Mills plant produced feed for livestock. It was a much larger plant than Lamkin's. There must have been six or eight floors in their plant. Each floor had a different function of the production. I was hired on as a utility man, which meant I would do whatever I was assigned to do. Mainly, at first, I was to work on each floor to sweep up the dust and clutter.

The floors were accessed by way of a man-lift, a sort of conveyor with steps and handholds that allowed employees to ride up or down to the various floors.

On the first floor was the production line. A bin that weighed the feed accepted the appropriate sack or bag. The filled container (sack or bag) was released by a foot-activated pedal to fall onto a conveyor. The conveyor carried the sack or bag to the sewing machine, where a technician would guide the product through the machine. Then, the container would fall onto another conveyor that would slide the product onto a table where a worker would stack it onto a pallet (for storing in the warehouse) or onto a sturdy piece of cardboard (for loading onto a boxcar). The easiest runs for the production crew were when we were running pellets for the bulk trucks. Then, the feed would dump into a large bin, which would be taken by forklift to the waiting bulk truck.

We worked 24 hours a day, with weekends off.

We had come to the conclusion that the neighborhood where we had moved was not where we wished to stay. We found a really nice house closer to Texas Christian University (TCU). As I remember, it was on University Circle, just off Granbury Road. The drive to work was no longer, and the house was much nicer—as was the neighborhood.

We hadn't been able to get a telephone, but we did go to Montgomery Wards to purchase a clothes dryer. Two in diapers made the trips (although necessary) to the clothesline drudgery.

One morning, about 2:00 a.m., I was taking some trash from the building at General Mills to the incinerator. There was a short stair-landing from the door leading out to the incinerator. The door was one of those necessitated by a fire code. As I look back at it, the door-closer was not working. I had put off eating (would it be called supper or breakfast?) until I took care of this chore.

I dumped my load and climbed the few steps to that landing that allowed me to reenter the building. I reached my hand across the door to pull it shut. Without warning, a sudden burst of wind slammed the door shut. . .on the last joint of the middle finger on my right hand. It was as clean an incision as a door could make. I never even opened the door. My finger was bleeding profusely, and I was hurting.

I guess it was the night manager who took me to the hospital. There, the wound was cleaned and dressed. Some locally applied anesthetic reduced the pain. I was in the dirt of a feed mill. Catherine had no idea of my situation. We had no phone to alert her. We were blessed to have some old friends, Herman and Peggy, from Howard Payne, who had also come to Ft. Worth for seminary. They did have a phone. Early (actually, later) in the morning, I called to see if Herman would tell Catherine, take her out to pick up the car, and care for the babies until she got back home. What a friend!

What a trouper Catherine was. She arrived at the hospital without panic. I would have surgery later that day to add some more natural-looking profile to my wounded finger; then I would be allowed to go home.

The surgery resulted in my middle finger looking like a hammerhead shark. But, I wasn't bleeding anymore and was able to be at home. I can't remember how many days from work I was permitted. I do remember that I was scheduled to conduct my first wedding.

Max and Lera Jane were from Agee. How would they take me with that wounded digit? When we got to church the Sunday after the accident, they assured me that it was no problem to them if I felt like doing it. We did it.

I went back to work with a blood-stained bandage on that finger. What I had to do wasn't endangering my healing. Mr. Black visited with me about compensation from our insurance. I can't remember the amount, but I do remember that it was used to buy the kids a swing set. The healing wound didn't affect the assembling of that set.

It was a set that had two swings, a coaster, and a slide. Our kids gave it a thorough working over. We kept that set through three moves.

We learned that a third child was coming to join our family. We had been using a friend of Dr. Coleman. Dr. Bell had been in school with him and was practicing in the Mid-Cities area. The trip from our part of town to his office was not that bad, probably 20 minutes or so according to traffic.

Dr. Bell arranged for our child to be delivered at the All-Saints Hospital, which was not far from us, and we had explained that Catherine delivered in a rush. After bedtime, near 10:30 p.m., Catherine began delivery. We still didn't have a phone. What to do? Couldn't keep that baby from coming. It must have been God's grace that I was able to find a neighbor who was still up at that hour. He was doing some work in his garage. I explained our urgency. Would he call Herman and stay with our kids until Herman could get there? It was a desperate leap of faith. He agreed, and we rushed to the hospital.

The nurses at the hospital thought we were exaggerating. We explained to them what history had revealed to us. Catherine delivered in a hurry. Finally, they got with it. I remember hearing one of the nurses say, "I don't know the gender, but it has black hair!"

I had no more than gotten seated in the waiting room when Dr. Bell (still in his street clothes) told me that we had a healthy son. Kirby Dale Craig was born June 22, 1961.

We considered ourselves some sort of model for family planning. Three kids in four years.

Our 1957 Ford had served us well. Looking back, I am ashamed to admit that I allowed my indiscreet passion to influence me again. The 1957 Chevrolet was so sharp looking. I had to find some rationale that would permit me to trade in a car with no major problems for another of the same model. I couldn't find adequate rationale, but made the trade just the same.

1957 Chevrolet

This was another car I should never have gotten. There was no valid reason for getting rid of that '57 Ford. We had had no trouble with it. I did let it get low on antifreeze and had the hoses freeze, but I got that fixed. The overdrive wasn't working well, but it was really just an extra.

I couldn't get that '57 Chevy out of my mind. I caved in to lesser values, and sought out some place where I could manage a trade. I did. Catherine never complained although I am sure I gave her ample cause.

It was a very nice car. A sort of emerald green. It didn't have that fancy chrome that the Bel Air had, but it had the same sporty lines. It had low mileage, with an automatic transmission. Still no a/c.

The work at General Mills was covering our living expenses, but those hours were keeping me from my reason for being in Ft. Worth—seminary. I kept my eyes and ears open for some job that had the hours that would allow me to get into school again.

In the rush just before Christmas, there was an ad for help at the Green Stamp Redemption Center. In those days, Green Stamps were given as a bonus and incentive for buying at various stores and businesses. When a book was filled with these stamps, folks would bring it to the redemption center to turn it in for some treasure. The number of filled books determined the quality of the treasure.

The job was part-time during the day. I was assured that, after the Christmas holidays, I would be considered a regular employee—still part-time, but with guaranteed hours each week.

My job was to help fill orders. We had enough warehouse to house the various items up for redemption. An order would be handed us, and we would trace down the desired item in the warehouse and get it up to the customer at the front. Compared with General Mills, it was light work and much less strenuous.

Mr. Black couldn't complain when I told him why I was leaving. He remembered that I had taken that job with him originally with the understanding that when I was able to find work that would allow me to go to seminary, I would take it. So, I did.

Christmas was a busy time at the redemption center. I was even given some overtime hours. It looked like I would finally be able to get into the seminary.

We loaded our three kids in the car and took off for Baytown and Highlands (not 15 miles apart). Catherine's folks lived in Highlands. Mine in Baytown. The holidays were hectic fun. Momma Bea's house was filled with her yet unmarried kids, ours, and Linda Rae's (Catherine's oldest sister). After the holidays, we returned to our cozy house in Ft. Worth, and I reported for work on Monday.

When I checked in for work, I was very rudely surprised. The management told me that I would not be needed after all! Here I was with a wife (the best), three kids (without question, the best), rent, and no job. I scheduled a meeting with a financial officer at the seminary, to explain my hopes and the reality we were facing. He was sympathetic and encouraging with my situation. The best counsel he could give me was to go back home, where I was known, get my finances manageable, and then come back and enroll here.

The counsel, although on target, was hard to take. It seemed that what we had planned could not come about. We explained our situation to our landlord. Catherine's dad had a one-ton, box-bed, truck. My brother, Randy, agreed to drive it up to our place in Ft. Worth, where we would load our stuff. Catherine and the kids would drive the car on down to Highlands, where they would stay with her folks until Randy and I got our stuff moved in. My folks had found a house in Baytown where we could live while we worked things out.

I called the church and explained to Chock what was happening. Could Randy and I spend Saturday night with him? I would explain our dilemma to the church on Sunday morning. Chock agreed although we hated to have to part.

The church understood and sent us on our way with their blessings.

It was cold and windy when we drove the truck into the drive of that house on Adoue. Randy and I unloaded the stuff (Catherine and the kids were still in Highlands). We did what we could to make the house appear livable. . .even putting up the TV antenna (what was cable TV?).

The house was old and set on piers; the wind literally whistled under and through it. We did have one of those Dearborn heaters that resisted the chill. It was not all we wanted, but it was our new home.

I immediately began looking for work. I got notice that a road crew was looking for laborers, and I went to the site to apply. I was hired and showed up to work the next morning. Some of the men I was working with were instructed to carry some reinforcing rods to the forms where cement was to be poured. The rods weren't heavy, but cumbersome. I thought I would take a clue from what the other men were doing—so I carried the same number of rods I noticed them carrying.

Our crew-boss confronted me, "Is that all you can carry?" I was shocked. I was doing just as the other men were doing. Still, he said, "If that is all you can do, go pick up your check."

That was the only job I was ever fired from. I felt worse than bad, and couldn't understand why my doing what the others were doing was not good enough to satisfy the boss.

We had joined Second Baptist Church in Baytown. My family all went there. Second was a vibrant church. Word about my situation somehow got around. I was introduced to Quinn Belt. Quinn was a deacon and—as I was to find out through many subsequent experiences—a very good man. He owned a company that did concrete work. He was willing to take a chance on me even though he knew I had just recently been fired.

I was grateful, and determined to prove myself to him. I began by digging beams around forms that would become the foundation for a new house. I learned how to put those rebar rods (much like the ones I had gotten fired over) into the beams. I helped as we leveled the grade for the cement (about four inches of cement). When the cement was poured, I worked with the others to pull and push the heavy mixture to grade (Horace did the straight-edge work). I hammered the boards around the beams, so no honeycombs would develop as the cement cured. I learned to jitterbug the cement so that "butter" would rise to the surface for easier finishing—butter was the mixture on cement and sand without the rocks. It made the finish smoother.

In time, as I proved myself, Quinn let me finish smaller jobs, such as patios and sidewalks.

That relationship with Quinn was supportive, not only in taking care of living expenses, but in restoring my confidence.

A friend of the family was moving his family to Tennessee to prepare them for ministry. Their vacated house became available for us. It was in the old neighborhood where my family lived when we moved from Cedar Bayou. Same floor-plan. Their garage had not been turned into "The Boy's House." With the good work with Quinn and now this better house, we were feeling very good.

I don't know how a church in Waller County got my name. I was invited to come to Shiloh in view of a call (to become their pastor). Shiloh was on a main farm-to-market road. It was just outside the campus of Prairie View A&M. The church has just completed a parsonage. If we were invited—and if we accepted—we would be the first family to live in this new house. They would furnish us the house and pay us $100 per week.

The church asked us to come. We were excited to accept their invitation. Raymond and Bud came down in two stock trailers to move us up to Shiloh.

Before we leave this chapter, a quirky word about that '57 Chevrolet. Ray saw it and, like I was with my attraction, had to have it. He had a '52 Ford convertible. The body was maroon, and the top was white (the colors of the high school in Baytown). Ray would give me his car and take up the payments on mine.

The convertible was just a brief interlude, but deserving of mention. However, that '57 Chevy will come back in for a short exposure later.

1952 Ford Convertible

This car occupied only a very brief chapter in our life. It was sharp, but maybe not altogether suitable for a pastor. We drove it only a short time before Ray contacted us (we had moved to Shiloh) and wanted to give that Chevy back. He had done some work on the engine (those Chevys had a really hot V-8). Ray had installed a hopped-up cam and a speed-shift transmission.

In this condition, it was really not a suitable car for a preacher.

I got introduced to the Dodge/Chrysler dealer in Waller. Suggitt Brothers had been there on the corner at Highway 290 for some years. I took the Chevy in to see what kind of deal we could make. I came out with a bright red Dodge Lancer. This Dodge deserves its own chapter in which I'll discuss our life in this latest car.

1963 Dodge Lancer

This was our very first new car. We got to put the first miles on it. The Dodge was a brilliant red, all over. It was a four-door with standard transmission. It had the radio and heater, but still no a/c. We were very proud of it. As a precaution for the kids, we had plastic seat covers installed over the upholstery. That plastic left little diamond dimples on the exposed parts of your skin as you sat and sweated. It also had a slant-6 engine.

When Shiloh called us to come preach for them, the membership knew that I would have to do some additional work to care for the needs of our family. The Philip brothers had a massive dairy operation just up the road from the parsonage (the parsonage and the church were on the same acre of land). I was offered a job there.

I had no experience in a dairy, but was willing to learn. Initially, I would come on around 7:00 a.m. The morning milking was just finished, and cleanup was required. The milking barn was on a concrete floor that dropped down four inches from the entry walk. The cows would walk in from a holding pen and place their heads in a trough where a bucket of feed had been deposited. There were 12 stanchions, which meant that we could milk six cows while getting the other six either ready to milk or ready to turn out.

The milkers were operated by vacuum. Most of the cows had such healthy bags that the vacuum was all that was needed to hold the milker up in place. Sometimes, it was necessary to hang the milker on a strap about the cow's middle. You couldn't let a milker lose vacuum, or all the machines would drop to the floor. I was learning all this. When milking, you kept a close ear on the sounds. Any squeak would sound an alarm for immediate attention. When the milkers did drop to the floor, it was more than a mess.

None of the cows had been potty-trained. Cleanup included washing their refuse out the door and down the alley. The milkers had to be washed.

After cleaning up, the cows had to be let out to graze. The Philip brothers had a dune horse that was used to herd the cows out to graze—and back to milk. We called him Dune.

Besides the milking, I helped with the farming necessary to produce the feed for this large herd. I learned how to operate a tractor. We planted oats, corn, and milo (for silage), and we bailed hay.

Raymond and David were the perfect pair for their operation. David knew cows. Raymond was keen on the farming side. I worked with both men.

I got to the place that they trusted me to actually milk. When needed for the morning milking (we started at 3:30 a.m.), I remember how David would go into Mrs. Philip's house (probably around 5:30 a.m. or so) and come back with a couple of cookies and a six-ounce (small) Coke. It picked us up for the remainder of the morning.

In addition to the pay, I could have all the milk we wanted. It was cold, right out of the cooler where it was kept for transport.

We enjoyed our little house. It had a nice living area, a kitchen large enough to cook and eat in, two bedrooms, and a bath. It smelled so new! We had to buy a window air conditioner to combat the heat and humidity. There was no gas or butane to heat or cook with. The house was all-electric. We hadn't expected—nor had they—that heating that little house with radiant electric heat would be so expensive. We even had the Rural Electric Association (REA) come out and check our meter and service. We did put insulation in the attic. It helped some.

We got our mail at the mailbox down by Highway 1488. Kenneth Gruner brought the mail. The kids loved to meet him at the box. That meeting was a thrill for Ken as well as our kids. They would pick "flowers" (quotes because some were blooming weeds) and present their bouquets to Gruner (they always called him by that last name). It was an adventure for them and him. Play, or whatever, would be interrupted with the cry, "Here's Gruner," and the kids would run down to meet him. Kenneth always saw to it that each of the kids would get a piece of mail. Junk mail took on this expression of grace.

The local paper did a feature on Mr. Gruner. He asked if our children would pose with him for a featured picture. We have a copy.

Although we never did have an over-supply of cash, Catherine always managed for us to eat well and for the kids to dress well.

Mr. Bud and Laverne lived just behind us, through a cattle guard. They had cattle. It was regular for them to graze right up to the fence that bordered our place and theirs. Mr. Bud and Laverne were sweet to our kids, giving them candy and such.

Kirby was small, even for his age. He was dauntless. We once caught him walking through those grazing cattle on his way to Mr. Bud's for a candy bar. He couldn't have been over three years old. The cows didn't seem to mind. Kirby had Hershey's on his mind.

During one of my visits to prospects, I met Grady. He was a single young man managing a ranch not far from our church. Grady had a little dog that took up with us. When his job necessitated a move, Grady asked if we wished to keep Blackie. It was a good time. Blackie stayed with us for a long time. More will be mentioned about her in subsequent chapters.

Since the work at the dairy was so close to our house, I could let the kids take turns riding on the tractor with me. Did it thrill them or me more? Each kid would sit on my lap as we bounced across the field. They loved those rides.

Often, I would borrow a tractor and mower to cut the grass around the church and parsonage. When I borrowed from Quinn Ray, we would drive over to his house (back roads, unpaved), get the tractor, and find a place for all three to ride on the way back home.

Blackie would always accompany us. She would sometimes be agreeable to riding on the tractor with the kids. Other times, she would run along with us. Although she was an exceptional pet for us, she was not that discreet about her morals. After her second litter of pups, we took her to Prairie View for the vet to "fix" her. During her recovery from surgery, she escaped and ran home. She was still wrapped, around her middle, with bandages. The kids held the idea that she had been cut in two by some mower, and sewn back together at this dog hospital. Kids!

Bang's disease was very contagious among cattle. Regulations required that testing be done periodically. If there was any suspicion that a cow tested positive, the entire herd would have to be tested until no positive reactions were noted.

The Philips had a very large herd. Using Dune, we would crowd the cows into a corral. Each cow would be urged into a squeeze chute where she would be immobilized. Her head would come into a device that would hold her steady. The vet would take a sample of blood from her jugular vein. My job was to hold her head up so the vet could get his sample. It sounds crude, but I had a plier-type device that would grasp the nostrils and let me use that leverage to hold the cow's head up.

After the sample was taken, I would remove the device from her nose, release the constraint on her neck, and open the front gate on the chute. Normally, the cow would back up and welcome the opened front gate—and exit with appreciation. Normally, that is how it would happen.

Number 75 was not a normal cow. She was a very athletic Holstein. She was muscular and hard-headed. She had been through this testing routine before. With some prodding (facilitated by an electric prod), Number 75 came into the chute. We squeezed her on the sides. Her head came through the constraint on the front gate as it should. She cooperated with the vet and me—to a certain degree.

When the sampling was completed, I released her nose and relaxed the constraint on her neck. That constraint was enabled by a 4 x 4 timber that opened with the gate. When I relaxed her neck, Number 75 backed up. . .as she should. Then, however, she stuck her head back through the neck constraint. I had taken the chain that secured the front gate off its nail. I reached around to kick her nose, expecting that she would back up and then calmly walk out the gate. Instead, Number 75 hit that gate like a linebacker! The gate flew open and that 4 x 4 handle caught me squarely behind the left ear. I passed in and out of consciousness. McWilliams took me by ambulance to the hospital. It appeared, after a thorough examination, that I had suffered no real harm. There is some tangible benefit to having a hard head.

I went back to work at the dairy, but began having recurring headaches. Further exams showed no cause until a perceptive doctor asked about my education and my work. When he learned that I was working as a dairy hand even though I had a college degree, he believed that I was suffering psychosomatic headaches. His prescription was for me to find another job.

It was difficult to explain to the Philip brothers. It was difficult for me to understand. I did go into town and was provided a job with the local Purina franchise. My headaches never recurred.

The church was doing well—so well, in fact, that we had to add on. We agreed to add a wing that would serve as the fellowship area, with additional Sunday School rooms. The auditorium would be extended toward the road. We would do as much work as we could. Marvin Parker would be our professional guide and contractor.

Marvin was a gifted carpenter. He just seemed to know what to do and how to do it. It was remarkable how he decided to extend the auditorium. The front of the church had a short steeple and a short porch before the entry. Marvin told us that we could cut that front loose from the existing building, pull it to where the extension would be placed, and pour the slab between the newly moved front and the existing building. It worked!

Our kids were being spoiled by the folks who extended such love to us. Without being disrespectful, they called the folks by their first names. They knew who to sit with to get gum or cough drops.

I came to the sad conclusion that we could not pay for that new car—it was just too much on a limited budget. Catherine has always been supportive. We agreed that our only recourse was for me to return the car to Suggitt Brothers. We got all out stuff out of the car, and I drove it into town. Jimmy was understanding. He couldn't give me any money back, but would accept the car—and its indebtedness—without any hard feelings. I didn't have a way to get back home. I didn't know how we would get around. It was a sad time for me.

Looking back, it must have been God's directions that led me by Gertrude McWilliams's office. We had met when I officiated at some funerals at one of their places. Gertrude listened as I poured out my recent problems. She offered me a chance to work with them, and gave me a ride home.

There ended our adventures related to that '63 Dodge. However, our adventures were far from over.

1958 Chevrolet Bel Air

We had to find something for transportation. A daughter of one of the church members was selling her older car. We found a way to buy this '58 Chevy. It had been well-cared for. It was what we needed at the time.

I was no longer working at the Purina store. The McWilliamses had graciously given me a chance to work with them. They had a far-flung enterprise. They were mainly known for their funeral home. In addition, they had a flower shop. They dealt in insurance and, in addition to all that, they provided an emergency ambulance service. I can't remember the rate, but I would be paid by the hour—except when opening and closing a grave; that was a set rate.

The first night I worked with them (seemed that most of our work was at night!), Glen came to the parsonage to see if I was available to help open a grave at Kirby Chapel. The soil there was tough. There was a lot of iron ore in the ground. Digging by shovel and pick was near-impossible. They had bought a portable posthole digger. Glen would position the bit and dig as deeply as needed. The ground quickly ate the edge off the blades, making it very necessary to replace them regularly.

Finishing out the grave had to be done by hand. The digger couldn't square out the corners and the floor had to be leveled. Oscar, an ageless worker, and I would get into the hole and beg—with pick and shovel—the dirt to give up and give in to our efforts.

That grave at Kirby Chapel was the first of many with this benevolent family that was helping meet our basic needs.

Shiloh was near halfway between Waller, where Gertrude and Alton were and Hempstead, where Bob McWilliams had the funeral home. I was blessed to work with both families. It was not unusual for a grieving family to need a minister to conduct the service for them. We made an inside joke at the McWilliams's places that we were the only funeral home that offered one-stop-service. The preacher would help prepare the body for the service, open the grave, conduct the service, and close the grave. I got used to changing from my suit—most of the cemeteries were deep enough in the country that I could find a place to change clothes. More than once, though, I managed the change in the back of the equipment truck.

We had some harrowing experiences running the ambulance. One of the saddest came just after a funeral at Waller. I had just gotten out of the shower at Alton and Gertrude's house when the phone rang. There had been an accident in the south part of town, just over the railroad tracks. The ambulance was gone on a call. We responded in the funeral hearse.

What we found, when we got to the scene, was a very tragic story. A group of boys had been dove hunting. As they sat around joking, as boys do, one of them raised his gun to feint a shot. He apparently did not know that there was a bullet in the chamber. The blast immediately killed the boy at whom the joke had been intended. So sad.

My experiences with the McWilliams family challenged while enriching me.

Everything seemed to be going so smoothly at Shiloh. One of the members of the school board was active in our church. He had been in the area for some time. In fact, his father had been on the board, and he had graduated from high school in Waller. In our church was a relative newcomer. He decided to run for a position on the school board. It happened to be the same position for which our longtime member was seeking reelection.

The high school had asked if I could help them in an emergency. Their enrollment had exceeded the required ratio of students to teachers. They asked if I would teach a class or two and be on campus, so that they could be in compliance. The church agreed that it would be fine. I did come on board with Waller High School.

I got the craze for small foreign cars. My rationale was the great gas mileage they afforded. I was willfully ignorant of the costs of maintenance and so forth. The '58 Chevy had served us admirably. My obstinate determination was the only reason for trading it in.

We went into Houston and made a deal (maybe suffered a deal) for a 1963 Simca. It's likely you haven't heard of such a car.

1963 Simca

As I recall, the Simca was being marketed by the Chrysler dealers. It was a French car. It had a rear engine, five-on-the-floor transmission, four doors, and leatherette upholstery. It would hold our family fine. Catherine had been very patient with me through all this.

The men at the church gave me a hard time about it. The car was so small, but I remember one of the guys saying, "Well, from the dash to the trunk, it is close to normal." It would have to do for us.

We arranged for someone to care for the kids while we drove into Houston to complete our shopping for Christmas. Foley's was still in operation downtown at that time, although I hated to drive into downtown Houston. We found what looked like the perfect thing for our kids. It was called a climbing tower. Of course, it required assembly, but it looked really good as it appeared in the model. We agreed that our kids would get a lot or service out of it (proven to be a gross understatement!). We bought it, but how would we get it home? Creative and willing staffers helped us lash it to the top of our little Simca. We must have looked like some oddity driving with that overhanging box atop our diminutive car.

I had to assemble that thing so it would be ready for the kids on Christmas morning. I had the set of instructions, a box-full of stuff, and only the front porch light to see by. Their response made any effort worthwhile.

The climbing tower stood about eight feet tall. There was a ladder to climb up to a platform where you could slide down a pole, like a fireman.

It was the perfect complement to their swing set (which we had brought with us from Ft. Worth).

It didn't take long for our kids to find some creative ways to enjoy that climbing tower. Maybe among the first of their innovations was to climb up the pole you were supposed to slide down. It made a great vantage point for their creative observation.

The competing school board candidates and my working at the school created a volatile mix. Some of the folks, who had been silent when we discussed the situation at the school, had become unhappy. They felt that I should be full-time at the church. What had been a healthy environment became lethal.

I saw that I was the center of the controversy. The best option, it appeared to me, was for me to resign. It was a sad time. We had made so many deep friendships at Shiloh. Still, we felt that leaving was what we had to do.

By now, Cheryl was in school. She was an eager student. It was a sobering experience to see our little girl jump onto the bus when it stopped to pick her up.

Cheryl had always been like a little mother. Cathy was in her first grade. Mrs. Strawn, the first-grade teacher, was stern and intimidating. Cathy cried often, and Cheryl would console her. Joan, Cathy's mother, said that Cathy couldn't have made it through the first grade if it hadn't been for Cheryl. All three of the kids had Mrs. Strawn as their first-grade teacher.

I had the income from the school, so we had some budget. We did need a place to live. The Tompkinses had a house they had just vacated for a new home they had built. We made a deal for that house and the five acres it sat on.

It was a frame house, with three bedrooms. The attached garage had been converted into a family room. This family room was a good two feet lower (since it had been the garage) than the front room. There was a fireplace in the front room. . .and that led to a lifelong addiction. We loved to sit and gaze into that fire.

Dwayne had offered to cut us a cord of wood and deliver it for $25! See if you can find a deal like that anywhere nowadays! Many happy hours were spent lounging with the kids and wife before that cozy fire.

We were not exactly "in the woods," but we were in the country. One day, as Catherine was carrying some trash out the back, she saw a snake. With controlled determination, she used a hoe to cut that snake into pieces. No snake was going to be any kind of threat to her kids.

We had to have a well dug for this house. Previously, Burgess's house and that of his mother were served by the same well. Calvin dug the well for us. Somehow, the well ended up on the adjoining property. We had a mess to deal with.

The Perez family bought the house next to us. . .the house where Mrs. Elise had lived. They would buy our place and solve our problem about the well. We sold, but then we had to find another place to live.

Rental property in Waller was at a premium. All we could find was an old frame house that had been vacant for years. It sat on a street adjoining the school ground, so it was a great location. The house, though, was not great. It sat on beams. Over the years of neglect, some or the beams had sagged, leaving large gaps between the floors and the walls. Rats, not mice, had taken the house for their own. For the brief time we lived there, we fought those rats with vigor. They seemed immune to our best efforts. We couldn't live there for long.

The Harrises had a trailer-house just south of town. They didn't use it that regularly, and they saw our desperation. We were so happy to leave the rats behind and move into a place where we could feel some safety.

There was not enough room in the trailer for all our stuff, but there was a barn where we could store what wouldn't fit in the trailer.

We had to burn our trash (there was no garbage pickup). There was a 55-gallon barrel that served as an incinerator. We knew to be very careful, for fear of a fire that would go out of control. Despite our most cautious efforts, we did have a fire. A piece of burning garbage dropped out of the barrel and raced into a storm despite our best efforts to fight it. The volunteer fire department came to our rescue. It was like a charred funnel that led from a small beginning at the barrel, to a wide expanse. No damage, other than to my ego and some grazing land.

I was working more regularly with the McWilliamses, and still teaching at the high school. We really wanted our own house. We learned of places in Houston that would build on your lot. That interested us. Gertrude McWilliams had a lot that we were interested in. I worked out a deal with her about that lot. She would give me the lot in exchange for labor. I would be credited with $35 for each grave I worked. We agreed on a price, and I continued to work.

The lot was just across the road from the parking lot at the stadium. It was a choice location. We agreed with a company in Houston about building that house. How excited we were! The house would be a colonial-type, with columns on the front porch. It would have red brick and a charcoal shingled roof. The side-entry garage allowed an extra window on the front side. It would have three bedrooms (one for the girls, one for Kirby, and one for us). Two baths, a separated dining area, and a sunken living room completed the floor plan. We had them include a majestic corner fireplace (how we had missed that while in the "rat house" and the Harris's trailer).

Christmas came while we were watching our first new house going up. We got each of the kids a bicycle. I put them together and hid them in the barn at the Harris's. What a world those bikes opened for our kids!

Our house was nearly finished! We couldn't wait.

My work at the school was on what they called an "Emergency Assignment." If I wished to continue with the school, I would have to go to college to complete some of the requirements for a degree that would qualify me to teach.

The income from the school was only for the 9 months of the school year. I had no income for the summer. The father of one of the boys I taught in school had just opened a Texaco station on Highway 290, just as you leave town. Dan, the father, wanted to experiment with making it a 24-hour service station. I needed to work, and he gave me the chance.

I came to work at 11:00 p.m. and worked until 7:00 a.m. I had enrolled at Sam Houston for six hours so I could be qualified to teach in September. I met a carpool in Hempstead at 8:00 a.m. to ride the 50 (or so) miles to Huntsville. I couldn't keep my eyes open. One regrettable day, I was seated in the back seat between two ladies. One of those ladies was the wife of our county sheriff. She was wearing one of those blouses without sleeves. . .you know the kind. I couldn't help falling asleep. As I did, my head fell over onto her bare shoulder. That was bad enough, but when they awakened me as we came into town, I became aware that I had slobbered all over her arm! How sweet of her to recognize my weariness, and not sic her husband on me.

We survived that difficult summer. I was given another year to teach. All three of the kids were now in school. Catherine had taken a part-time job as a teller at The Guaranty Bond State Bank in Waller. One of the special thrills for the kids was to go see Mom at the bank.

With my teaching job secured for another year and with Catherine's extra income, we felt we could get a car that would be more comfortable for us. I went to Jimmy Suggitt. Could I buy a car from him if I had it financed elsewhere? He was agreeable to that arrangement. We drove down to Highlands to visit with Daddy Ray's mother. Big Momma kinda kept the books for the family. She would let us have the $2,700 we needed to buy the car. With that check in hand, we went back to Waller to close the deal.

We sold our little Simca to Buster Davis. We were saddened to learn that not long after he bought the car, Buster swerved to avoid hitting a dog and was hit—head-on—by a truck. The Simca was brought back to Waller on a flat-bed truck.

I drove with Frankie to pick up our 1965 Dodge Coronet.

1965 Dodge Coronet

How proud we were of this new car! It was a sort of coffee-tan, four-door with automatic transmission. The upholstery was cloth (much more comfortable to sit on), and we had air conditioning!

While the dealer tags were still on the car, I drove it to Dermott, Arkansas. A friend from Howard Payne was pastor of a church there and invited me to come lead them in a revival effort. Dermott was in the Mississippi River Valley. I never had seen such tall cotton or soy beans. In our part of Texas, a good crop might be waist high. Here, the growth was above your head!

The McWilliams family made it possible for me to work with them on a full-time basis. I helped with funerals (one-stop service). I worked in the flower shop (Delta Faye was an artist with flowers). I worked with Glen in the Western Auto Store.

We were in our new house now. The McWilliamses lent us a piano so that—for the housewarming—we would have some furniture in that sunken living room. The very first time I mowed our backyard, the mower threw a rock through the patio door.

We went into the woods to dig up oak trees for replanting in our yard. We erected a basketball goal in the vacant lot next to ours. The swing set and the climbing tower were in their proper places in the yard. We were all enjoying this fine new place—even Blackie.

Blackie did cause us some tension with the neighbors. She loved to dig, and the soil there was easy to dig in. In addition, Bennie and Mr. Ferguson both had gardens, which meant tilled soil that was even easier to dig in. Blackie was incorrigible. None of our discipline did any good about this vice of hers.

We stacked our firewood along the property line between us and the Fergusons. The girls invented delicious pies from the loose soil there—decorating their creations with chinaberries.

As mentioned earlier, our new house was just across Field Store Road from the parking lot of the football stadium. After a Friday night game, our kids would be up early on Saturday morning to search for money that had been dropped from seats in the stadium. This Saturday morning adventure didn't wait for breakfast. They were up and at it early.

Now that they had wheels (their bikes), nowhere in Waller was inaccessible. Our girls found confederates in the McCaig girls. Kirby had a firm friendship with Brian Dennison. Their bikes really made it handy for them to hurry their finds from Friday night down to the S&N Grocery, where they exchanged their treasures for a variety of candy and such.

Wherever the kids went, Blackie would go. The door at S&N was activated by a switch on the floor-pad. Pressure there would open the door. Blackie would lay on that pad as she panted and waited for the kids. The loudspeaker would request, "Craig kids, get your dog off the door."

Blackie would go with us, and the kids, to the baseball and softball games that were so close by. She became a favorite of many of the fans. I have seen them, the fans, feed her popcorn and even gum. Don't know if such was healthy, but Blackie never complained.

While working with Glen, I got very interested in stereo components. We had a special cabinet built into the corner of our den, across from the fireplace. The amplifier, turntable (yes, that is one of the ways we played music in "the old days"), and tape player were housed in that cabinet. The speakers were installed in the ceiling. The sound was awesome! Kids we had taught in Waller High would come to visit, and would marvel at our stereo sound.

Technology had just come up with a four-track tape player that could be installed in a car. It was a hit. In only a short time, the four-track was upgraded to eight-track. Everyone had to have one. I replaced my old reel-to-reel player with a Roberts, that would also record—and play back—eight-track cartridges. I was able to record eight-tracks for car players. Almost overnight, I became an industry. It started with kids I had taught at school. Word got around, and most every evening I would be cutting a tape for someone. The kids would go to sleep to Credence Clearwater Revival, Hank Williams, polka music. . .some variety!

Cheryl, with encouragement from Mrs. Pecht, was promoted from second to the third grade. Cheryl was bright and eager to learn. Her birthday being in September made her closer, in age, to the kids a grade ahead of her. This promotion was a good thing.

Mrs. Roberts (the wife of our high school principal) was Christi's second-grade teacher. She recognized the gifts in Christi, and was a great encouragement to her. With some coaching, Christi was able to, as a second-grader, recite the 23rd Psalm at Parents' Night during Vacation Bible School. She amazed us and those in attendance.

Kirby had become tight with Timothy Friedel. Timothy lived in Hockley. One afternoon, Mrs. Friedel called to ask Catherine if she knew that Kirby had come home with Timothy. We knew he was late coming home, but never suspected that he would take it upon himself to invite himself to spend the afternoon with Timothy.

I was given the opportunity to reopen a little gas station that had been unused all the time we had been in Waller. Roy Cook had the Texaco bulk plant in Hempstead. He would see that the property was shaped up, install up-to-date gas pumps, and install a lift for us so that we could do oil changes and grease jobs. It was a challenge, but also an opportunity. We agreed to work with Roy, and concluded our longtime arrangement with the McWilliams family.

Glen let me make a deal to mount and balance all the tires he sold at the Western Auto Store. That would give some additional income.

With fresh paint and new pumps, we opened "Craig's Texaco." There were only three pumps—two regular, one extra. It almost seemed too small to amount to much, but with the Lord's help, we did well there. Friends we had made at church and through our association with the McWilliamses came to us for service. Kids and families from school would come. We added on a cover over the grease-bay so that we could work in rain. We did a lot of minor mechanic work.

Roy was also a salesman for fertilizer and feed. He would stop by every morning to fill his tank before hitting the road.

We were, so far as I know, the only station that featured kid-service. Our kids loved the air gauge I provided for each of them. Each had an oil rag in a hip pocket. Customers seemed to enjoy them climbing onto the hood to clean the windshield. As a reward for their service, we would walk across Highway 290—being careful of the busy traffic—for a French pastry and a chocolate milk. Wonderful help.

In my determination to be an effective service, I attempted to get into the wrecker business. Like too many of my decisions, I was too smart to listen to good advice. Rather than creep into this new business, I jumped in. I bought a Holmes Wrecker. It was "the top of the line." That move was only one of too many that I would like to do over.

The station, with that arrangement with Glen, was doing even better than I could have hoped. Few believed that we could make a living out of such a tiny, inconvenient place. The 1968 Dodge Charger was something to see! I had my eye on one and took the necessary steps to take it home.

1968 Dodge Charger

The Charger had a classic body style. It was green on green...a sort of (as Delta Faye said) "sewage green." The top was vinyl. Ours had a split bench seat with the gear shift on the steering column. The split seat allowed for three passengers (when needed) to sit in front. It was a very classy car.

We drove it down to the station, where we changed out the factory-supplied whitewalls for some more suitable to it. Of course, we installed the latest eight-track player. There was not another car like ours in town.

The '65 we traded in was in more than excellent shape. One of my students, who was going to Rice University, bought it.

The kids were all in school. As mentioned before, each one of them had the same teacher, Mrs. Strawn, for the first grade. Kirby had met Robert Hebert (French pronunciation) in school. They became good friends. Robert thought he had found a girlfriend. After class one day, he saw his "girlfriend" (they were only in about the third grade) walking down the hall with another boy! And, he had his arm around her waist! And, she wasn't resisting! Robert confided in Kirby (get ready for something profound), "Kirby, you better watch for girls. Girls are tricky, they are tricky."

Pat, Robert's mother, was the pianist at church. Richard, the youngest of their three boys was, as we said in the country, a toot. She had him sit beside her as she played. We always marveled that she could tend to him (keep him under control) while never missing a note. An exceptional mother and pianist.

I had been invited to return to Agee for a revival meeting. We (me and the people at the church) wanted Catherine and the kids to come up for the weekend. They could take a bus from Waller to Waco. It was not that far from Agee to Waco. I would pick them up and we would finish the work at Agee and drive back home. I was more than anxious to see them. I arrived just before the bus was scheduled to get there. When it arrived, the kids just came bounding off it. Catherine looked as if she'd spent a hard day in a steamy kitchen.

The kids had loved the bus. It had a restroom in the back. They wore out the aisle tripping back and forth to this mobile novelty. They enjoyed that bus ride much more than their sweet and loving mother. After the Sunday evening service, we drove back home.

Rodney was on a fine arts team for summer missions with the Student Division of Texas Baptists. They were assigned to work on the beach at Surfside (near Freeport, Texas). We arranged to go visit with the team, and dressed the kids as if for church (cute dresses for the girls, matching pants and shirt for Kirby). The team was really good. Rodney played the guitar, and the team sang contemporary gospel music.

Their setup was right on the beach. After the service, our kids begged to wade in the water. It was inviting, and the beach had made the waves shallow. We allowed them to take off their shoes and wade. In less than a moment, they were soaked. We should have known that the combination of that warm water and their adventuresome spirits would be too much to resist. We drove back home with them in wet clothes, but not feeling—at all—apologetic.

My brother, Richey, was with the James Roberson Evangelistic Team. They were working in Pasadena. It was our best chance to catch Richey doing what he did so very well. I got Dale to cover for me at the station. Dale had come to Waller to do music for the Waller Baptist Church. He was also going to school over in Brenham, at Blinn Junior College.

We were excited about the trip. I wanted to show off my wonderful family—and my fancy new car. In those days, seat belts were not mandatory. Catherine was in the front with me. The kids were roaming in the back seat. I remember that Christi was standing just behind me as we drove.

Traffic forced us to stop on the Pierce Elevated in midtown Houston. It was normal traffic for that time of day (just deepening from dusk to dark). We were idling, waiting for the traffic to move. Without any warning, we were thrust into the car in front of us! A driver, under the influence, had hit us—at 55 miles per hour—without ever touching his brakes! Not only did I hit the car just in front of us, but the car in front of it also. The impact was so severe that it broke the engine loose from its mountings. The manifold was broken, so that there was no muffling the engine. The window next to Christi's face just exploded.

How we came through that with no significant injuries can be attributed only to God's grace.

A local wrecker towed us away from the scene. I called Dale to bring our wrecker and tow us back home.

The Charger was totaled. There was not another equal replacement. We looked at a Chevrolet. We finally, although not completely satisfied, settled on a 1970 Charger.

1970 Dodge Charger

We grieved the loss of that Charger. This new one was different. It was a nice blue with a white vinyl top. The split-bench we preferred was replaced with buckets. There was a console that separated the seats. Two people were all that could sit up front. We did change out the tires from the '68, and we resigned ourselves to be satisfied with this car. It did not dissolve our grief.

Catherine was having a really bad time with her sinuses. We found hope in nearby Columbus. Catherine went to keep her appointment with the doctor. As she was entering the road, a car side-swiped her passenger side. Gratefully, she was not hurt, but the car was.

We were supplied with a loaner while our car was being restored. Somehow, the paint sample got messed up. The car came back blue, but darker and not as vibrant. We took it anyway.

The station had to be open every day. I was being challenged by what God intended for my next adventure. I knew that God had called me for special service. This was all a necessary interlude—a time of learning and maturing.

I was given the opportunity to buy the station and the building it adjoined. The other building had a second story, which had been vacant for some years. The lower floor had been a sort of variety store. All the stock had been removed.

What was I going to do with this other building? I had a better arrangement with Texaco now that I was an owner. I had to tap my brain for some use of this other building. I was expanding too fast. I could see some opportunity, but didn't see that realistically. I also entered an arrangement to operate another station. This was a larger building, but sold Sinclair products. I had hoped to service commercial traffic out of this additional location, since it offered more room than what I had at the Texaco station.

God was working on me. I could feel His tug to follow Him into a fresh adventure. At the time, Christian coffee-houses were in vogue. These were places where an easy atmosphere encouraged talking and community. The upper floor of this newly acquired building would serve well. With some of my station help, we built a modified handball/racquetball court in one corner of the building. It was a new and challenging sport for our population. Kids loved it. We also painted the entry door a bright red, and lettered "The Upper Room" on it.

I began doing my Bible study up there in "The Upper Room." The local kids took to it. We had some local talent that provided live music for us. We were having good crowds. One downside was a misunderstanding with some of the older folks. They complained to me that I was taking from the church. In fact, we were another face of the church.

It was a time I felt great freedom in sharing verbal witness to my faith.

The McWilliams family in Waller was having to get out of the emergency ambulance service. Regulations, collections, and age were all valid factors in that decision. I made arrangements with the Waller Volunteer Fire Department to take over that service. I had earned my Instructor's License so I could qualify members of the Fire Department to work in the ambulance. The McWilliams family provided a new 1970 Dodge for conversion into an ambulance. I would keep the ambulance at the Texaco station and at my house. Frank installed an emergency phone next to our house phone.

Richey had met Lyn, and they were to get married in Lubbock. Gertrude thought taking that trip in the '70 model Dodge would be a good "break-in" for it. Randy was going to ride out there with us. . .possibly even help drive.

It was our first trip to Lubbock. We drove until past exhaustion. We stopped in Sweetwater and as we were gassing up, I asked the operator how much further it was to Lubbock. His estimation was that it was 200 or so miles further on! The trip, there and back, took all our energy and stamina.

We converted the '70 Dodge from a standard station wagon to a serviceable ambulance. I provided white coveralls for us to slip on when we got a call while at work at the station.

Catherine was riding with me as we were taking Mr. Purvis to Navasota. It was a calm transfer, no lights or siren. It was a clear day, with the sun shining brightly. Mr. Purvis was sleeping on the cot in back. The way the cot was situated, his head was just behind the back rest on the front seat. Just as we were pulling under the overpass into town, Mr. Purvis exploded into an unexpected sneeze! We were quickly refocused on our task.

Catherine and the kids were very involved with Waller Baptist Church. I have never questioned their fullest support of me. I talked with Catherine about what this next step might be. We prayed for guidance and timing.

I made arrangements for the station to be opened. I would go to church with my family this Sunday. When the invitation was given at the close of the service, I came to the pastor to say that I was accepting God's invitation to return to service. At the time, I interpreted it to enter the field of evangelism. When I was introduced to the congregation with my decision, Catherine came to stand with me. One by one, from various places in the auditorium, the kids came to stand with us. What affirmation!

Roy agreed to buy the station and that adjoining building. The Sinclair station reverted back. The Fire Department designated members to drive when the ambulance was needed. I am not sure that everyone involved understood and/or supported our decision. We were doing what we had to do.

Waller Baptist Church afforded us our first opportunity to preach a revival. My brother, Rodney, agreed to come lead the music. I can't remember the results, but I know we appreciated the opportunity.

The McWilliams family helped with a revival out at Reid's Prairie. Delta Faye played the piano (multitalented lady). Bob led the music. We had the chance to do some preaching out in the basketball arena at Prairie View. Jerry Young helped get some "name" people for this meeting. We had some folks who had worked with Billy Graham. I was, just a little later, invited to come to Big Spring to work with a friend we had been very close to in Brownwood.

With only what came as "love offerings" from these revivals, I couldn't keep up the payments on that '70 Charger. Joe McArthur was the pastor in Hockley. He had a Renault and would trade it (with no payments) for my '70 Charger. It seemed the thing to do.

1969 Renault

Joe was happy with the trade. He was taken with our Charger. The 1969 Renault was a rear-engine car with a standard transmission. It could accommodate our family, being a four-door. We had made the trade because we wanted to be out from under the payments on the Charger, and we hoped for better gas mileage.

I was scheduled to begin a series of services in Big Spring. That trip would give me a decent chance to see how the Renault did on the road. I stayed at home as long as I could and left quite early on Sunday morning to get to Big Spring for their morning service.

The meeting went well at Big Spring. Catherine and the kids sent me letters of encouragement. It was so sweet to read how they prayed for me each evening before bed.

Cheryl was ready to learn to drive. It was convenient for us that the parking lot was just across from our house. We could safely practice on that surface. Cheryl caught on to the standard transmission pretty quickly. We taught all three kids to manipulate a standard transmission. Our thinking was that if they learned how to handle a manual transmission, then they could drive almost anything.

On one of our practice sessions, I felt confident enough in Cheryl's skills that I let her drive across the road. With me in the passenger seat, I was helping her watch traffic. As we pulled up to the road, I looked to our left and could barely see an oncoming car in the distance. I said something to Cheryl about giving it some more gas to hasten across the road. She floorboarded it! We did a super "wheelie," but got across the road before the oncoming car had any chance of hitting us.

The girls were playing softball. Kirby was playing baseball. We practiced football in the lot between our house and Field's Store Road. Two of the kids would be on defense. I was the all-time quarterback. . .throwing the passes. The kids would alternate between offense (one receiver) and defense (two defensive backs). We designed routes such as "The Fly," "The Zig," and "The Down and Out." We could have been fierce competition for any other four-man team.

Randy had earned his private pilot's license after his discharge from the Marines. Reggie was playing a freshman game against Texas Tech at Lubbock. Lyn's parents lived in Lubbock. Would we be interested in flying with Randy and Connie out to Lubbock? We would watch the game, spend the night with Lyn's folks, and fly back to Waller the next morning.

Sounded acceptable to us. We drove out to Bud Adam's ranch (yes, the man who owned the Houston Oilers). There was a landing strip there. I knew Adam's manager, and had his OK for us to land and take off from there. Close to time, Randy landed his rented plane, and we flew—uneventfully—to Lubbock.

All I can remember about the game is how windy it was there. Reggie played, but I can't remember if they won or not. We rode with Lyn's folks to their home, which had just recently been completed. The lawn was not fully grown-in. That information will be important to this story. Jody, Lyn's mother, drove us out to the airport. An oncoming weather front prohibited us from being able to take off. We waited until assured that there was no way we could fly out that day.

When we agreed to the trip, we had arranged with Mrs. Howell to stay with our kids overnight. We knew her from the library, and fully trusted her. We called home to let Mrs. Howell know that the weather was keeping us in Lubbock for at least that day. She could stay with the kids, which helped our discomfort (what else could we do?).

Jody took us back home. To ease our conscience for the trouble we were becoming to Jody and Pete, we asked if there was anything we could do that would be a help. Pete showed us what he wanted done with the new turf in the yard.

We ended up having to spend two nights in Lubbock. That experience was more regret than pleasure. We were more than thrilled to see that little Renault sitting there beside Adam's airstrip. Mrs. Howell was gracious—and we're forever in her debt.

We pledged never to make such a trip again when the weather could stymie us so.

Our time with the Renault didn't last that long. Joe had to bring the Charger back. We had no choice but to take it back. We eventually sold the Charger and traded my wrecker for a 1972 Chevrolet.

1972 Chevrolet

We knew that we were moving back to Baytown. Second Baptist Church had asked me to join them as their Staff Evangelist. We understood that it would be an unpaid position, but the affiliation with the church should influence some opportunities.

I can't remember just how we disposed of that 1970 Charger, but I do remember that I drove the wrecker into a Chevrolet dealership in Houston. By phone, I was assured that they would accept the wrecker in trade for a car.

That is how we came to own a '72 Chevy. It was a bare-bones model as far as accessories go. It was a V-8, with automatic transmission, air conditioning, but no power steering (go figure). It was a General Motors blue with four doors.

We were, now, completely free of the several businesses we had involved ourselves in.

We found a house, 136 McArthur, in Baytown. The house was in the Brownwood subdivision in the part of town known as "Wooster." It was the biggest house we had lived in. Because Brownwood was in an area that had been hard-hit by an earlier hurricane, the owners were willing to sell the house far below market value.

Catherine's Dad, Ray, lent us his truck again, and Randy drove it up to help us load for the move. The plan was for us to load up the truck, which Randy and I would drive to our new house. Catherine would finish other stuff that would fit in around her and the kids in the car. She would be bringing Blackie.

We were scheduled to close on the day that we moved. It was getting too close to our scheduled closing time, and Catherine hadn't arrived. When she did arrive, she looked exhausted. Blackie was a nervous wreck in this move. Catherine had stopped to allow Blackie to get a drink. . .and the little dog fled the scene! After more than several minutes of beckoning, Blackie agreed to get back in the car. We closed—sweat, exhaustion, and all.

The house was a pleasure for us. It was situated on a lot and a half, with mature trees. It had three bedrooms and two full bathrooms. In addition to the den (beautiful fireplace), there was also a formal living room. The attached garage was side-entrance. Much of the interior consisted of beautiful knotty paneling.

We decided, before school would start, to take a little trip. We hadn't gone anywhere, as a family, for the years I was so involved in various businesses. Reggie, a younger brother, was playing football for Arkansas. Our plan was to drive to Texarkana where they were playing Southern Methodist University (can you figure that one out; with SMU being in Dallas?). After the game, we would drive through some of the places we had served, such as West Bowie. Before returning home, we would spend some time on Lake Brownwood. We thought it would be a sweet trip. . .and informational for the kids.

One of the very first things I did after we got this Chevrolet, was to install an eight-track player. It fit under the dash as if designed to be there.

We drove to Texarkana for the game. Had to park on the street. The Razorbacks won the game. We visited for a few minutes, and went to our car. We had been broken into! Some thief had forced open the vent window on the driver's side, opened the door, and made off with our eight-track! You may have experienced that emotion of violation.

We continued our trip. The church at West Bowie was in bad repair. There was no one left from that congregation we had served some years before. We were not sure that the church was even active any more. The kids were interested, but it wasn't much to see.

We rented a cabin on the shores of Lake Brownwood. We ate at Underwood's, a famous bar-b-que place. We went by the college (a university by now) and showed the kids where we lived when Cheryl and Christi were babies. We swam in the lake.

We came back home to get the kids into school. Cheryl was in high school. Christi was in junior high. Kirby was finishing elementary school. Cheryl played coronet in the band, and was excited to be going to the same school where her parents had graduated. She intended to be a twirler, just as her mother had been.

Christi would play the alto sax. She fully intended to become a twirler in the famous Lee band when she got into high school.

Looking just a little ahead, Kirby would become a drummer.

The Brownwood addition had been hard-hit by the last hurricane. It was suffering with subsidence, a condition that exists when substances are pumped from beneath the ground causing the ground to sink. With the pumping of oil, and our water coming from wells, the surface of Brownwood had sunk seven feet from the time the first houses were built there.

The city had approved and built a perimeter road that included most of the homes in the subdivision. There were several homes that were on the bay side of the road. Studies had come to the decision that a seven-foot elevation would keep the bay out of the homes in Brownwood.

It didn't take us long to meet our neighbors. On our left, the house was vacant. On our right was a man who had been a football hero in his day. Just across the street, we met the Sanchez family. Sylvia was in high school with our girls. Raymond was just younger. "Tic" was close to Kirby's age. Mrs. Sanchez was a single-mom. We became very close with the family.

Second Baptist Church was very evangelistic. As a part of their strategy, they had purchased a tent, which they erected at various places around town for the purpose of conducting evangelistic services. As Staff Evangelist, I was responsible for these meetings. A young man we had met in Waller, Kenny, came to spend the summer with us. He would help in the prayer walks preceding each meeting, help erect the tent, and work with us in the music (Kenny was an exceptional guitarist). Catherine and the kids were more than supportive, and participated to some degree in each meeting.

We were busy that summer, but we were not receiving any money. Looking back, I cannot explain how we were able to live for those three months with no more than $500 for the entire time! We must have experienced a modern-day application of that widow whose pantry never ran empty. It doesn't compute, but we experienced it—with no deprivation.

I realized that something had to be done. God, who had graced us during this summer, convinced me that something else was necessary. I had to swallow some pride. I had thought that, now that I had committed to this ministry, I would have what was needed to care for my family. I called on old friend, Sid Guest, who owned a filling station in Baytown.

We had gone to church with Sid and his family at Stewart Heights. I knew him to be a good man. Sid preached when asked. I told Sid my situation and asked if it could be possible that I work for him. Sid took a chance on me. . .much as Quinn Belt had done some years before. I went to work the next morning at Sid's service station.

I knew about pumping gas, washing cars (Sid insisted that there be no streaks on the glass), and changing and mounting tires. When Catherine needed the car for her errands and responsibilities, she would drive me into town (about six miles through a part of the refinery). Otherwise, I would take the car in.

I had not been there a week when Sid asked me to drive Mack Smoke to his office so that we could mount a new set of tires on his car. Mack was the Director of Missions for the Bay Area (Baptist churches in the area). As we drove, I just asked Mack about his student work at Lee Junior College. Mack fell silent. Had I said too much? We drove on in silence and I brought his car back for service.

Later, that very day, Mack called to ask why I had asked about the student work. I could only answer that I was making conversation. Mack went on to say that, only that week, he had been given permission—and budget—to employ a part-time Baptist Student Director. Would I be interested in considering it?

What an experience of unexpected grace! I went from unemployed, to under-employed, to employed. I was not yet aware of all that was included in the door that had begun opening.

I was given an office in the Bay Area Baptist Building, just adjacent to the campus of Lee College. With this position, I was granted association with pastors and staffers of cooperating churches. This opening door was opening other doors.

I had been invited to return to Waller County to lead a revival. A threatening hurricane was in the Gulf. Landfall was uncertain. . .except we knew it would happen. I hurried home to prepare the house for the possibility of some encroaching water. Estimations were, if we got any water, that no more than a foot of water might flood us. We put up our furniture so that it might escape any flooding.

The storm didn't come in when expected. I had spent the night at home, in case of an emergency. When it appeared, the threat had passed, we took the furniture back down, and I prepared to go back to continue this series of meetings.

Sometime during the early morning, Raymond called. Water was coming up the drainage ditches. As we were talking, I heard our commodes flush. I quickly awakened the kids. Catherine was up with the phone call. We hastily dressed and hurried to the car. By the time we got to the car, we were wading water near knee deep!

The hurricane had come ashore down the coast near Freeport. The storm surge had sent our bay over the perimeter road. Except for a very few houses on the upper elevation of the subdivision, all of Brownwood was flooded. A worker with our Civil Defense said it was like submerging a bucket in a bathtub. The water in our house was 15 inches deep. All the furniture we had put up on blocks was saturated.

All we could do was wait as the pumps drained the excess water from around us. We all gathered at the convenience store up on the road to share care with one another.

When we were allowed to go back in, we were saddened by what we found. As I entered the house, I could hear a buzzing. I followed the sound from room to room until I came upon the foot-pedal to Catherine's sewing machine. It had been flooded and shorted out. The carpet was all soaked. The beds ruined. The washer and dryer, and refrigerator, were all ruined.

We couldn't find Blackie when we were rushed to leave. Looking around after the water went down, we found her on the outside cabinet of Rudy's air conditioning unit, next door. At her age and with the trauma of the flood, her heart had failed.

We had lost much of our furnishing and our loyal pet, all in one sad day.

Kirby was a great help to me during this time. Our house was bigger than any we had previously lived in. We had to replace the roof. Would it be possible that he and I could do that? I had some limited experience from the expansion we had done at Shiloh. Economics forced us to try. Daddy bought the shingles. Kirby and I put them on. Remember now, Kirby was only in junior high at this time. Great help.

During this time, I was also working at Central Baptist Church in Baytown. As I remember it, I was a sort of Associate Pastor. We, at Central, were wanting to reach out more aggressively into our community. One of my assignments was the development of our bus ministry. Our normal procedure was to provide the "bus kids" with a worship service more tuned to their ages and experience. However, occasionally we would take our "bus kids" into "Big Church." I remember sitting with a young Mexican boy. He was sharp (never underestimate how much these kids take in). He whispered to me, "Where is Jesus?" We had tried to get across the point that Jesus is present in our worship. He was expecting to see a tangible presence.

Billy Tate was our pastor. He had a 1965 Buick. It was as big as a bus. He made us a deal for it (seems we were always getting a "deal"). All I remember about this car is that it had a wrecked driver's side front fender and that we made a short trip in it to The Valley and into Mexico.

We replaced the fender with one (of a different color) that we got at the junk yard. It fit fine, but clashed with the white of the remainder of the car. No matter, we drove down to spend a brief time in Los Fresnos. Our Baptist Student Union (BSU) group had stayed there, at the church, when we were down for a mission trip at South Padre. The pastor let us stay in the fellowship building. The kids were so anxious to get to the beach. We got the ultimate of sunburns there! Kirby was so badly burned that the skin on his stomach just peeled! The pastor suggested aloe vera, and that greatly reduced our suffering, and hastened our recovery.

On this trip, we tasted our first fresh-from-the-field broccoli. What a taste! We got to pick some oranges from the orchard.

We never complained about our "two-toned" car.

Randy and Connie needed a car. We agreed to let them take up the payments on our 1972 Chevrolet. . .and they did. Therefore, we needed to purchase a new car.

1972 Toyota

I seemed to still be obsessed with foreign cars. I thought what we lacked in comfort would be more than compensated by what we saved on gas. Without a trade-in to worry about, (Remember, Randy and Connie. . .) I found us a low-mileage 1972 Toyota. We, again, sacrificed air conditioning. We had bucket seats in the front, with a manual four-speed on the floor. It was a sort of dried mustard color.

Cheryl was rehearsing to get her driver's license. We wanted it to go well. . .and she did need some practice with a standard transmission. We had put the house back in livable shape. We did have flood insurance, and were able to replace the furnishings we had lost to the flood.

The roads in our subdivision were a safe place for Cheryl to practice. One day, we were practicing pulling up a slight grade. The perimeter road offered an ideal place. We pulled into a vacant drive on the bay-side of the perimeter. Some local kids were playing near that drive, and they discontinued their games to give us room. Cheryl put the transmission into first and started back up the slight grade. Not enough gas, and the car died, rolled back down the drive, and the kids went back to playing.

She started the car again. . .with the same embarrassing results. The kids didn't know whether to stay out of the way or continue their playing. The same scene was repeated at least three times. The car would roar to life. It would stall out on the way up the drive. The kids would get out of the way. Three times. Finally, she goosed it enough and we—and the kids—were relieved.

Cheryl had made the twirling line. Christi was determined to try out the following year. Kirby was drumming in the band at Baytown Junior High.

Catherine had enrolled in a shorthand course at Lee College. We thought that specialized skill might help with additional income if it came to that. She aced the course. We never were forced to use the skill she had mastered.

My position at the BSU (Baptist Student Union) had expanded to Director of Special Ministries. I was drawing a near full-time salary. In addition to being the BSU Director, I worked with hearing-impaired students, did some supply preaching and interim work, and some disaster relief work.

About this time, Kirby went exploring with his uncle Reggie. They came to a little creek and had to find a way to cross it. Reggie saw that he could jump across. It would be too much of a jump for Kirby, so Reg gave him a little help as he jumped. Kirby landed awkwardly and broke his right wrist. Of course, Reggie felt terrible. . .as if it had been his fault. Accidents happen.

We got the wrist set and, when the time came, went back to have the cast removed. Dr. Holsomback took me aside and confided that he needed my help with that cast. The X-ray revealed that the break had not healed properly. The wrist would have to be rebroken and set properly. I didn't know what all that involved, but wanted to do whatever I could to help my son. The doctor explained that Kirby would be under anesthesia and would not be aware of any pain.

We watched as Kirby went into that induced sleep. When he was fully under, we held him and forcibly rebroke that wrist. I can never forget that experience. Although he was anesthetized, his mouth flew open in a silent cry of intense pain. His eyes opened momentarily. It was, I think, the most traumatic thing I have ever experienced. In reflecting on that, I have a clearer appreciation for what our Heavenly Father experienced when He had to witness the suffering of His only Son.

Kirby's wrist healed fine, and he has had no trouble with it.

We needed a second car. With the kids in different schools, the girls involved in after-school activities (like band), and church, we needed sufficient transportation. Daddy had a very serviceable '70-something Chevrolet on the lot. We were happy to get it.

Mom and Dad went most weekends to watch Reggie play football with the Arkansas Razorbacks. Daddy would have me watch his car lot. I wasn't expected to sell anything, but greet "lookers" and accept payments (most of Daddy's sales came from him carrying the notes and the buyers making weekly payments). He paid me for that time. If I remember correctly, it was these weekends that purchased that second car for us.

Catherine has always been creative and conservative. We lived much better than our earnings would indicate. She sewed for the kids. She stretched the grocery budget. She found ways that we could afford what we couldn't have otherwise. The situation with Kirby's teeth is a good example.

Kirby needed braces. He had a marvelous smile, but some of his teeth were crooked. Catherine found a place in Houston where graduate dental students did dental work at a greatly reduced price. All work was done in the presence of supervisors. She arranged the necessary appointments to have Kirby's teeth straightened. That perfect smile that Kirby now flashes is due to his mother's efforts. That second car was proving indispensable.

I was asked to serve as interim pastor while the pastor search committee of First Baptist, Crosby, looked for their next pastor. It was a wonderful experience. So many fine people!

I was at Crosby for close to a year. Not too long afterward, Cedar Bayou Baptist asked if I would come preach for them while they were looking for a pastor to come in and attempt to fill the place that Brother Burns had occupied since the founding of the church. Brother Burns had been their first—and only—pastor for more than 20 years!

I was pleased, although surprised, to find several of my old friends and classmates among the membership. Quinn and Marie Belt had moved their membership from Second to Cedar Bayou. It was so good to work with them again.

Richard Steele, who I had met—and worked with—at ETBC, came as pastor. It is unusual for a pastor who is following a long-tenured pastor to stay for very long. Richard was the pastor at Cedar Bayou until he retired. . .over 20 years.

Both our girls inherited their mother's beauty. . .outwardly and internally. They were attractive dates, and the boys began calling.

I met Gary Fuller through one of the secretaries at Second. Gary's family had a Volvo dealership in Baytown. I had heard about Volvo's reputation for quality and toughness. Gary helped me work out an affordable deal, and the Toyota went as down payment on a 1974 Volvo.

1974 Volvo

We really felt something in this shiny blue Volvo. It was a four-door, with a standard four-speed, radio, and a/c. It was the classiest car we had owned. One of our first reactions was how much higher it was set off the road than any of our previous cars. It was pretty. It was tough.

The Bay Area had asked if our family would consider serving in a sort of resort area for the summer. The schedule would allow the kids to keep their obligations at school. The area was called Big Thicket Lake Estates. It was in Liberty County, between Dayton and Livingston. There were no deed restrictions in the subdivision, so most of the dwellings were trailers. Some of the residents lived there year-round. Others spent time there during vacations, spring breaks, and summer.

We were surprised to learn that the manager of the place was a boy (now a man) that I had gone to school with. His sister was a classmate of Catherine's. The family lived right down the street from the Princes in Highlands.

Sam, on staff at Second Baptist, lent us his pop-up camping trailer. Charles (our school-mate who managed the place) arranged for a place for us to park. We arrived after dark, but were able to get set up for a needed night's rest.

We found that we could meet most of the population at one of two places: either The Fun Center or the "lake" (quotes because it stretches the definition of a lake).

The Fun Center had pool tables, foosball tables, some electronic games (like pinball), and tables for cards and such. No one, except visitors and some adults, wore shoes. Billie tended the concessions.

We wanted to engage in as many relationships as we could. Our kids really helped. We didn't get good at either pool or foosball, but we tried. . .and met people in the trying. The local kids fought boredom. We used that situation to introduce engaging activities for them. We put up a volleyball net and imagined a court. Everything there, it seemed, was on a hill. Whenever that ball would hit the ground, someone had to chase it down the hill. We played a lot of volleyball.

Something they hadn't tried was "Capture the Flag." Sides were drawn. Each side had a "flag" to protect. The goal was to get to the opposing side and capture their flag. . .and get back to your side without being tagged. To add some adventure to the game, we titled it "Capture the Flag in the Dark."

Two stories come to mind. Henson was very athletic. He could run like a deer and seemed fearless. Henson was always, in Capture, on the offensive. After an attempt to get to the opponent and back without being caught, Henson was limping a little. When asked what had happened (remember, no shoes), Henson said, "There are some stobs out there." We could only imagine the pain of running—with bare feet—upon stumps.

We oftentimes played "Flag" on the same court where we played volleyball. One of our bunch we called "Tall Paul"—it was obvious that he was taller than any of us and that he was attempting to escape back to his side while avoiding being caught. He sprinted up the middle of the field. . .unaware of the net strung across for volleyball. He bounced off that net as if he were the ball. He wasn't hurt, except maybe for his pride, and we all collapsed laughing.

We were being accepted by the population at Big Thicket. Charles found us a vacant trailer that would be much more comfortable for us than the pop-up camper. It was more like a home.

How proud we were of our kids. They met these new kids with no reservations. It was so gratifying for Catherine and me to have our entire family so involved in ministry. You would have been so proud of the kids, as they sat on the platform of one of our largest churches in Baytown to give their slant on our efforts that summer.

School started, and we moved back to 136 McArthur. We drove the kids to and from school. Sylvia, from across the street, rode with us. Usually I would drive them in as I went into work at Lee College.

Christi surprised us by joining the golf team. I had been introduced to golf when leading a revival back at Shiloh. I was thrilled that Christi was interested. In fact, we got Kirby to play with us. Cheryl had gotten her driver's license. When she was still on her learner's permit, we would let her drive when we went into Baytown.

The road from our house into town went through the middle of a large part of the Baytown Refinery. The smell is one that you can't forget. Those early rides, as she was growing in experience and skill, were—to say the least—adventuresome.

Reggie had been influenced in his decision about which college to play for by Raymond Berry, the Hall of Fame receiver who played pro ball with Johnny Unitas at Baltimore. In Reggie's sophomore year, Raymond left for a position in the NFL, and Don Trull took over as receivers' coach. The impatient Craigs didn't think Reggie was getting to play enough. I am sure, as I look back, that our calls to complain to Trull may have worked more against him than for him.

Catherine and I were invited by Dr. Robertson to fly with him to a home game. He had a private plane. We were excited to go. That trip was my first in a plane equipped with an automatic pilot. Not long after we'd gotten to the flight path that would lead us to the airport at Rogers, Arkansas, Doc took out his paper and began reading. . .as if at home in his easy chair!

Frank Broyles was the legendary coach of the Razorbacks. We were privileged to eat with the team before the game. As we were going through the buffet, Broyles said a sort of generic "Hello" to Catherine. She said, "I don't believe I know your name." Innocent sweetness.

The Bay Area asked if our family would be available to work in Big Thicket again the next summer. We were happy to agree. With a little more time for planning and such, we were given a more comfortable house for our time in the Thicket.

We had pretty well decided (at least Catherine and I had) that we would not get another dog after Blackie's death. The kids were older now, and we didn't think we needed a pet. The kids didn't agree with our reasoning. One of LaDonya's dogs had a litter of pups. They were a cute blend of Border Collie and "whatever." We thought (emphasis upon "thought") that we had a clear understanding with the kids. I came home, after they had been at Momma Bea's, to find a cuddly little ball of black and white fur. I guess they knew we couldn't send him back.

The kids named him Elton. Elton John should have been flattered.

Elton moved with us for the summer at the Thicket. The house provided for us was a nice little cabin. We had air, inside plumbing, and sleeping room for all of us. The house was on beams, so Elton made himself at home under the front porch.

Our closest neighbors were an older couple who were raising their grandson. From what we learned, it was a sad story—in one way—and heroic in another. The baby had been abandoned. No one was certain for how long, but the grandparents found him in his crib crying his eyes out. He was decimated from abuse and hunger. He had a home now. We did what we could to be neighbors to this child.

It was easier, that summer, because we had some already established friendships. It was good to see these folks again. They did remember us, and we them.

I had found an abandoned motorcycle in one of the deserted cabins. It was partially disassembled. No one wanted it, and I was free to take it. I had always liked to tinker, so here was a project for me. The kick-starter could not be found. I reassembled what could be found. As I was tinkering with it one morning, spinning the rear wheel, the motor started! What a surprise! I now had a bike that would run.

Philip had an old scooter that needed a transmission. We could have the bike, and he had some parts if we wanted to try to make it run. It became a project that Kirby and I could work on. We also got it running! Now, we had transportation to wherever we wished to go in the Thicket.

In addition, we had gotten an old Buick that fit in very well in the Thicket. It was a faded blue, with four doors, and a muffler that wouldn't stay put. It fit well in the Thicket.

You didn't have to have a license to drive in the Thicket, since it was a private community. Both Christi and Kirby had learned to handle a standard transmission. Neither had gotten a driver's license. Both could, and did, drive that Buick while in the Thicket.

A youth group from Garland came to spend a week with us. Those kids were so envious of Kirby because he could drive a car! We got both Christi and him legal in time.

When summer band started up, Catherine would have to drive the kids (all three were in the band) back and forth. It was a strain on her, but she never complained. It was, as she saw it, expected of a mother.

I met George and Debbie at the lake. In that hot East Texas sun, the lounging in the water was not only a treat, it seemed a necessary coping activity. George was very good on the guitar. As we visited from day to day, I learned that they were engaged. I was honored when they asked that I perform their wedding ceremony. That would come at the end of our summer.

We would try a tent revival that summer. The Area provided the tent, and some flyers to advertise. We had discovered a talent in Daniel. He helped us with the music. The services were inspirational and effective.

The summer was over. We packed, and Catherine and the kids drove back home. I stayed to do the wedding; then, I packed that old Buick (even taking the motorcycles) for home.

Since Cheryl had her license, we were wanting to get her a car. She could drive herself to school and such. Her ability to drive, if she had her own car, would take a big load off Catherine and me. Daddy had a '72 Chevrolet Vega. It was a faded purple, two-door, with standard transmission. The Vega had a slanted four-cylinder engine in an aluminum block. Vegas were only in production for seven years.

The first night Cheryl drove the Vega to a football game, she decorated the car with some shoe polish and balloons, and burst off to the game. She gave that Vega a workout.

I was heavily engaged with my work at The Bay Area and the interim at Cedar Bayou. Events at school were keeping us busy. All three of the kids were involved in the band. Cheryl and Christi were both twirlers. We were proud that our kids were so well-liked. Both the girls were recognized in the homecoming court at that homecoming game. It was my esteemed privilege to stand with them—a beautiful girl on each arm—on the field as their names were announced over the P.A. As some wit noted, "Beauty and the Beast."

Shortly after this homecoming event, I got an invitation from The Baptist General Convention of Texas (now Texas Baptists), to come on board with them as a consultant in their Mission's Division. It was an unexpected invitation. We talked—a lot—about it. To accept it meant we would have to relocate. We had so many attachments in Baytown. Cheryl was to graduate in May. Christi had intentions of becoming drum major of the band. Kirby was entrenched with his friends in the area, church, school, and band. Both sets of our folks lived nearby. Still, we felt we had to consider it.

Darwin flew down to visit with us. He was the Director of the Mission's Support Section of the Mission's Division. Catherine and I met him in Houston. Our evening was cordial, with no commitments offered or made. As expected, the kids were anxious to learn all about that meeting.

Within a month, I was invited to come to Dallas (then office of the convention) for more talk. I learned that I would be recommended to the commission that approved any hiring. I went back home, excited yet anxious. I knew moving would be hard for us. I never questioned that we would do what we believed the Lord wanted us to do.

I was approved and began commuting. . .I think it was in March. Separation put a strain on our family. We have always been very close. I could only come home on weekends. . .and not every one of them. I endeavored to do all I could to make our move as pleasant as possible.

I began looking for a house in the Mid-Cities area of the D/FW Metroplex. Richey lived in the Mid-Cities and I thought being close to him might be good for us. Smithville was growing rapidly. It was just off the freeway and was noted for its school system. I went so far as to put down a deposit on a house that I thought the family would like. I brought them up to see the house. They liked the neighborhood, but not so much that house. The sales representative said my deposit could apply on any of their houses not already on contract. We looked at all of them and settled on the one on the corner of Collard Court and Main.

We closed on that house, and I moved enough bare essentials in that I could live there until we could all move in. We took the kids by (Christi and Kirby, Cheryl was graduating from Lee) to visit the school. Christi learned of "The Dixie Belles" and was determined to get into this elite organization. It was above-average. She put in her application. We (via Southwest Airlines) flew her in for the essential try-outs. We learned later that the Belles were impressed that a prospect would fly in for try-outs. She made it.

Before school was out, we flew Kirby up to help with the landscaping. Kirby had always shown a special interest in yard-work. In fact, while we were still in Baytown, he used some of the money he had earned to buy a riding mower for the larger-than-normal lot we lived on. Kirby and I designed flower beds and planted shrubs.

The very night Cheryl graduated, we moved. The Convention sent a truck to move our furniture and such. We packed our personal stuff into our cars, and drove into Smithville. Elton rode with Kirby and me in the Vega. The truck with our furniture would be there the next morning.

We knew we would have to have a fence for Elton. Our next door neighbor's brother was a fence-builder! Looking back, we are amazed to see these—even incidental and trivial—ways that God was caring for us. Our fence was built of cedar pickets. A couple of the pickets had knotholes near the ground. Elton utilized these as "peepholes," and could poke his nose through at the end of what seemed a hazardous run. Elton's great aspiration was to escape, which he did on too many occasions.

My work called for an extensive trip through south Texas with a representative from our national partner. We agreed that I would provide the transportation. Bob and I were coming into Alice, Texas, when the Volvo developed some trouble. I think it was with our fuel pump.

We made it into town, only to find that there was no place that had the part we needed for repair. There was, they hoped, a possibility that something could be done the next day. No luck. After spending more than a couple of days waiting, I arranged for a wrecker to tow us to Corpus Christi, where the car could be repaired.

I couldn't take a chance on having a problem like that again. The Volvo was, for that part of the state, too exotic. I would trade it for something that could be more easily repaired.

With the necessity of my commuting and the challenge of the largest metropolitan area we had yet lived in and the trouble I had just survived in South Texas, I drove the Volvo to the Ford dealership in North Richland Hills. I negotiated a trade (I never was very good at this) for a 1974 Ford and a 1972 Plymouth.

1974 Ford/1972 Plymouth

The Volvo gave us enough trading power to get us into these two cars. It was intended that the Ford would be mainly for Catherine's use. Cheryl had moved to Gayman, Oklahoma, and left the Vega with us (Kirby would buy it later, when he had earned his license). Cheryl had married Larry in the summer after her graduation. They moved to Gayman to go to school there. Christi was deeply involved with Dixie Belles and school. She and Kirby were both now in Richland High School. Catherine had to have something reliable for her chores and to get the kids to and from their appointments.

When Christi got her license, we realized that we had to find some transportation for her. A 1976 Maverick came to our rescue. I guess it was in commemoration of the Bicentennial, that the car was painted red, white, and blue. It was mainly white with a blue top and red striping. It had a six-cylinder, automatic transmission, and a/c. It submitted to Christi's direction. She imposed her personality upon that innocent car.

The Ford, for Catherine, was a blue four-door. It was a nice car, although it wasn't very long after we got into it that it had to have a valve job—which the dealership helped us with.

The Plymouth would be my work car. It was a two-door with a vinyl top. For whatever reason, the door on the passenger side wouldn't open. It was not that convenient to have a passenger have to slide across from the driver's side to get in.

Rodney and Janie had asked us to officiate their wedding. We drove the Ford down to Gun Barrel City for the wedding.

When I came to work in the Dallas office, I found a parking space within walking distance of our building. The space cost me $15 a month. It was on Olive Street. A few months later, our building relocated from that place across the street from First Baptist Church, Dallas, to the Annuity Building. Parking there cost me $60 per month! Not too long after that move, the Convention bought property next to the Baylor Hospital in Southeast Dallas. A new building—with parking provided—was built there.

Christi was given the opportunity to work with me during one of her spring breaks. During Staff Week, we would go out, as staff, to eat together. On this day, with Christi accompanying us, we went to a German restaurant. The meal was sumptuous. As we were being given the ticket, our waitress asked if anyone wanted a dessert. She went through the sweet menu. The item that made our mouths water (Christi and me) was the way she said, "Hot apple dumplings with cinnamon sauce." How we hoped the crowd would say yes. To our lasting disappointment, they declined. We had to go along. . .regretfully.

Darwin Farmer, the man who had brought me to Dallas, retired during this time. I had been given the opportunity to serve as interim pastor at Meadows Baptist Church in Plano. What a wonderful time that was!

Bill Ryan was one of the members at Meadows. He took me, one day, to visit some of his older relatives who lived on one of the "M" streets in North Dallas. I learned that these good folks had a 1968 Buick Electra in superb condition. They couldn't drive it anymore, and offered it to me. I couldn't pass it by. We sold the Ford and bought the Buick. That Buick made us feel like something quite special.

1968 Buick Electra

Our new (to us) Buick was the top-of-the-line in 1968. It was a four-door Hardtop. There was chrome everywhere. The only thing we added was a cruise-control. Like I say, it was in showroom condition. It was big and comfortable, and felt like you were sitting on a couch rather than a car seat.

Catherine drove it, mainly.

Christi had graduated, and was preparing to go to North Texas State (now University of Texas North) in the fall. Kirby was a year behind her.

Both the kids had found jobs at Six Flags Over Texas. A highlight for Christi was when a Hollywood celeb visited the park, and she was recruited to accompany him—show him around. Both Christi and Kirby worked at various places in the park. When Kirby was working on "The River," he loaded the boats; then—as the last boat departed—he would jump from the dock into the boat, catching a grip on the roof to steady his footing in the boat. On one trip (the jumping on board had become pretty routine) he jumped aboard, but his senior ring caught on a wire and almost pulled his finger off! He still has an impressive scar to this day.

Kirby had taken possession of Cheryl's Vega. He probably didn't drive it with the reckless passion that Cheryl did. It was good for him to get about. Kirby was a responsible young driver. After a late shift, he called to say that the Vega wouldn't run. I drove over to see if, together, we could make it run. Our efforts availed nothing. We would attempt to tow it home.

From Arlington, where Six Flags was located, to North Richland Hills was at least 20 miles. Much of the road was multilane freeways. We ventured forth. At nearly every intersection, when we would have to stop, the rope would break. We finally got it home. The rope was much shorter than when we'd started.

The motor had to be rebuilt. It was learning for Kirby and me. We did get it running again, but had lost our confidence in it. Kirby put it up for sale, and got more for it than he had paid Cheryl when he took it over!

Kirby, with money he had earned at Six Flags, bought a Dodge Cordoba.

Sam, a very good friend from Baytown, had moved to serve a church in Craig, Colorado. He invited Catherine and me to come work with them for a week in the late-winter/early-spring. I was, because of tight schedule, completing a conference in Amarillo. Catherine agreed to drive the Buick up to Amarillo and meet me there. We would then drive on to Craig.

It was Saturday afternoon when she picked me up at the Amarillo airport. The trip on to Craig was much longer than I had anticipated. And, we encountered snow! We finally arrived at Sam and Ruth Lyn's around 2:00 a.m. Sunday morning. Yes, I had to preach at 11:00.

Sam and Ruth Lyn saw to it that we had a great time in Colorado. It was our first time to ski (should I say, "attempt to ski"?). We had sore arms most of the week from pulling ourselves up after falls. We did learn that the snow was better higher up the mountain. We enjoyed it. When Sam asked, "Would you do it again?", we were unanimous in "Yes!"

We spent one afternoon snowmobiling. That was also a blast! At one valley in the snowy mountains, we spotted a large herd of elk.

Kirby was taking some of his schoolmates on a trip to New Orleans. His car broke down near Beaumont. Daddy Ray followed me in his car with a tow-bar so that we could bring Kirby's car home, and I gave him the Buick to complete his trip.

I had traded my Plymouth for a new Mazda. Yes, I had to answer questions from folks who wondered that if I couldn't find parts for a Volvo, what made me think I could for a Mazda? As you have surmised by now, my car-trading didn't have to make sense.

We had gotten addicted to a fireplace from our initial experience in that house we had brought from Burgess and Ellie. The house we had in

Smithville had an inviting fireplace situated in the wall by the patio door. We loved to burn it.

Finding firewood, without paying an exorbitant price for it, was our challenge. We scoped around the neighborhood for dead—or dying—trees. The family bought me a chainsaw for feeding this fireplace. Rob, a new neighbor from just up the street, shared our love for fire. He had a pickup, which made him a valued friend.

A local airport was near our neighborhood. There was a large grove of mesquite trees on their property. I got permission to cut some of these for our fireplace. It was, it seemed then, a really good deal. The "Miss Texas Pageant" was in Ft. Worth. Christi had a ticket to go there with friends. We should have time (I argued with her) to get some wood and still have plenty of time to get to the pageant. I made it hard for her not to agree with me.

We embarked on our mission. It began a soft rain. . .and kept it up. Of course, it never occurred to me to quit and go home. Just a little longer and we would have the truck loaded. Then, we could go home. We did get a load. It was gently raining, so we were soaked. The ground was spongy. The truck got stuck (couldn't say I got it stuck). We worked and worked. Jacked it up. Put wood under the tires. Nothing. The clock was ticking. Christi was getting ticked off. Finally, I walked up to the airport office and told them my problem. In what seemed like a flash, the man brought his tractor down and pulled us out.

Christi had missed "Miss Texas." It is a tribute to her character that she forgave me. . .although the incident has not been forgotten.

Cheryl had met Larry while in high school. We learned that we were about to become grandparents. Follow closely, for things get pretty complicated here.

My brother, Rodney, had a Volkswagen that had quit running. He wanted to be rid of it, and I rented a tow-bar and drove to Mt. Vernon to tow it home. With some tinkering, I got it to running, and drove it in some of my work assignments. I think I had dreams that this car would help with our economics (realistic thinking?). I did drive it on a trip to Abilene, and had some confidence (properly placed?) in it.

When Cheryl called to tell us that Matthew had been born in Liberty, Kansas (closest hospital to Guymon), we had to go see. As I remember, we scheduled a flight for Catherine to fly into Amarillo, where Larry would pick her up and drive them to be with Cheryl. Christi and I would drive the VW up there, and the three of us would drive it back home.

A terrible three-spout tornado had just devastated Wichita Falls. As we approached Wichita, the landscape looked unreal. It looked as if a plow had been dragged across the land. We drove through—carefully, and gratefully (that we had been spared this hardship). It was early morning, and we needed to stop for breakfast. We stopped at Doc's Coffee Shop in Vernon. It was on the first floor of the tallest remaining building in Vernon. We still relish that experience.

Doc's was genuine. None of the tableware matched. Cups were chipped. Everything was clean. Service was personal. We still laugh about the lady who went back into the kitchen to supervise the frying of her order of eggs. "You always overcook them," she complained to the cook! I think Christi got a large orange juice and toast for 75 cents.

Cheryl was a radiant mother. Little Matthew was precious. He did have a little issue with lungs, but was soon ready for home. With Cheryl's release from the hospital, we three drove (disregarding comfort) home to Smithville.

Cheryl's marriage to Larry was disintegrating. He, Larry, seemed consumed with selfishness. He refused to deal with his passion, and neglected Cheryl and the baby. One morning at work, Cheryl called to say that she had taken the baby and gone to stay with a good friend in Stillwater, Oklahoma. Would I come and get her and the baby? I left immediately. We got home safely, but with some uneasiness.

Larry called, all apologetic. "Would Cheryl consider a restoration?" Cheryl was optimistic and forgiving. She wanted a happy home. This attempt proved to be futile. Not long after, Cheryl called and asked if she could come home. We were happy to have her, but sad to have her in this circumstance. As I remember, I rented a trailer that could be pulled by our Buick and drove to Guymon to load up what was hers and bring her and little Matt to our home.

Cheryl has to be admired for the way she adjusted to such disappointment. She sold the rings Larry had given her. . .reminders of a sad past. She began to run and exercise. She got a good job in downtown Dallas. Catherine and I were thrilled to see her adjustment and improvement. We got to keep little Matt while Cheryl was working. Catherine was loving being Matt's grandmother.

The Volkswagen left us after several disappointing attempts to keep the fan belt on its air-cooled engine properly adjusted. I think we sold it for salvage.

During the very brief time that Cheryl had gone back to live with Larry, we sold our Mazda to him. It was a good car, gave us no trouble, and we hoped would help in pulling their marriage together. Vain.

During our time in Baytown, Cheryl had become very tight with Donna Yaw. They were about the same age. Donna went to Sterling while Cheryl went to Lee. They were together in Second Baptist Church. Donna's older brother was Bradley.

Brad was recovering from a disappointing marriage. Rosie Yaw, Brad, Donna's mother, and my mother conspired as to how they could get Cheryl and Brad together. Apparently, a major part of their conspiracy was prayer because Cheryl and Brad's love continues to endure, with four children and (at time of writing) 12 grandchildren.

Cheryl had become friends with Bobby Guenther while they were in high school together. She was lobbying strongly for Christi to accept dating with him. They did begin to date, and—before too long—Bobby was coming to Smithville to visit her and us. It got so serious that marriage became a consideration. Christi left North Texas, and she and Bobby were married in Baytown.

In the midst of all this, my new supervisor at the Baptist Building resigned for personal reasons. I thought I was next in line, as far as time on the job was concerned. I was disappointed, then, that I was passed over (since then, I have seen the gracious hand of God caring for me when I was not even that aware of it). I had been doing some interim work at Hebron Baptist Church, between Carrollton and Plano.

I was both surprised and pleased to find that Gerald and Mary, prominent leaders in this church that had been rural for most of its history, were classmates from Marshall! Gerald had an upper-management job with General Electric. Likely from his business background, he scheduled a meeting of the pastor search committee and asked me to sit in with them. After some brief formalities, I was handed a contract. If I signed that contract, I would become the pastor at Hebron. I signed. Accepting that church meant that I would have to resign at the Baptist Building. It had been a sweet time, but time had expired.

We put our house up for sale (the market was really good at that time). While waiting for it to sell, I had to find some way to do my work at church during the week. Kirby had traded his car for an old Pontiac convertible. Our attempts at restoration were futile. I would take it off his hands (so that he could be released to buy a serviceable car), and see what I could do about trading for something I could drive without depriving Catherine of necessary transportation back at home.

I drove to a used-car place over on Highway 121, just out of Lewisville. The best I could do was to make an even trade of my (formerly Kirby's) Pontiac for two motorcycles. I rode the Suzuki home, and rode the Kawasaki on a later trip. Neither of us was really happy about this arrangement, but we were willing to make it work. I have been, for most of our marriage, a challenge that Catherine accepted. . .and she still loved me!

I would ride the bike over during the week. Catherine would drive with me in our Buick on the weekends. Sometimes, we would stay with a family over Saturday. More often, we would drive over on Sunday morning.

It didn't take long for our house in Smithville to sell. We were blessed with enough over mortgage and closing to invest in a house in Carrollton. . .but not just yet. Hebron had an old house, a parsonage. It was much smaller, but Robert and Lucy were willing to let us store our surplus in their garage. Robert was an excellent carpenter. With the church's endorsement, he took the large front porch into the house as an extra closet. . .which did help some.

Elton made the move with us. He was a challenge to keep in the makeshift fence I had thrown up for his abode. I was, at that time, attempting to run.

I had a course around the neighborhood. Part of the neighborhood was still rural. Just adjacent, were large and expensive homes in a classic urban setting. As I was jogging, I suddenly heard "clawprints" on the pavement. Elton had escaped, and come to join me on what remained of my run.

It was sad when I found Elton, sometime later, dead in a field near our house. I buried him near the house.

With the help of our realtor, we did find a house in Carrollton. It was one of those "Zero-Lot Line" kind of neighborhoods. It was a three-bedroom house with two full bathrooms. It had a two-car garage that faced the street. There just wasn't much lawn. It fit our budget and was in the neighborhood where we had been called to serve.

We seemed to do some "prettying-up" at every place we lived. We wanted to take some of the bricks that matched our house and make flower beds. We were probably the oldest couple in this new neighborhood. We had asked the developer if we could scout around for leftover bricks that could be used in our flower beds. He gave us full permission. We had a wagon that we could load with these bricks, and we began walking through the subdivision (it was growing rapidly). We got a call from the local police. Someone had called them to say that "an elderly couple was going through the neighborhood stealing bricks." Our developer let us off.

While I was on an extended road trip and the kids were in college, Catherine drove the Buick down to spend some time with her folks. That old Buick had a Rochester four-barrel carburetor on the top of the intake manifold. That carburetor had the fuel filter screwed into the front of it, which was just above the manifold. Those manifolds would get red hot with extended driving. It was not that uncommon for those filters to sometimes leak. When they did spring a leak, the gasoline would drip out onto that hot manifold. You'll likely have guessed where this is going.

As she was driving on the loop east of Houston, a car honked for her attention. Catherine learned that the gas had ignited, and the car was aflame! She pulled into the closest gas station (how grateful we were that an exit was that close). The fire was extinguished, but the car was totaled.

The sadness over the loss of the car was compensated for by the deep gratitude that our precious Catherine was not harmed. The car was towed back to her parents' house. We had to make some arrangements to get her home.

With some settlement from insurance, we got a 1972 Buick Century that Daddy had on his lot.

1972 Buick Century

Had we not been in such a situation (without a car, away from home, needing to get home) we may not have selected this car. Oh, there was nothing wrong with it, but it certainly wasn't our Electra. It was a light green two-door. It had an automatic transmission and a/c. The tires were only fair, and the hubcaps were those small "bottle-caps." It ran well, and would suffice.

We were so glad to get back home.

We had put together a gazebo kit in our backyard—it gave us a distinctive look. We also fenced in the back with a shadow-box cedar fence. Joe worked for Texas A&M in one of their nurseries. Their mission was to develop plants that grow naturally in Texas soil. Joe helped us get some of the trees and shrubs that we wanted, to dress up our yard.

We had one of the coldest winters in a long while during this time. Snow and ice made travel hazardous. . .and ill-advised. Kirby had met a friend at Baylor who needed a ride to the airport. She was from Vermont (I think). We started out. All along the route were cars that had spun out. We took our time, were blessed, and got her there—and got ourselves back home—without anything worse than a case of nerves.

By now, Cheryl and Brad were married and living in Baytown. Same with Christi and Bobby (we have since started calling him "Bob"). Kirby was about to finish at Baylor. We were feeling at home in Carrollton.

The church was doing well. Gerald and Mary, who had been so influential in the revival of the church and in getting us to come there, had moved (job-related). As we visited around the area, we were blessed to meet some very quality folks who were Baptists and graduates from Baylor. They were a part of a network of Baylor folks who were living in this Metroplex area. Eddie and Susan knew Tracy and Karen. . .who knew Mark and Mary Kay. By God's goodness, they began active participation in our church.

The folks who were there, with the exception of Gerald and Mary, were related—distantly or more closely. They were fine, friendly folks. They were pretty well satisfied with the way things were at "their church." We felt that we were compelled to be a force in the community that was changing and growing around us.

The original building was a classic. It was a red-brick structure with towers on either side of the entry doors. The windows were beautiful stained glass. There was no paved parking. There was no running water in the building. Between the building and the busy road was an old frame building (it was the old school building) that served as a fellowship area.

The original auditorium had been designed with balconies around the perimeter. With time and a decrease in attendance, the balconies had been sealed off—giving the auditorium the appearance of a single-story facility. There was a baptistry behind curtains on the platform where the pulpit stood (that pulpit was a classic of oak).

As we began to grow, we recognized that we needed additional space. We worked with the Baptist General Convention of Texas to get some plans and assurance of volunteer builders for our project.

How would we pay for this new facility? Texas Baptists then had a program they called, "Together We Build." It was designed to challenge people to both give—initially—and pledge to continue to give for three years, to meet the budget requirements. We had a very good coordinator. The blessing of God was evident when our coordinator said that, based on previous and extensive experience, we just couldn't raise what we needed. Well, we surpassed our goal! One family, alone, pledged $10,000. . .and paid it before the first of the year!

Based on our "Together We Build," the church qualified for a loan from the (then) Church Loan Corporation.

Our new building would attach to our present facility—on both floors. We would include restrooms and plumbing for a kitchen. The nurseries would be relocated to this new building.

Johnny Cartwright was assigned as our Mission/Builder. Excitement was high among most, but anxiety was present among many of the old members—as it was bigger than any challenge they had undertaken. We were amazed—and still are as we reflect on that time—at how everything just seemed to come together. Jim, a licensed electrician volunteered himself to take care of the electric. I have no idea how much money his experience and labor saved us.

Hebron was on a hill. Beneath that hill was formation after formation of white rock. The plans called for 13 piers to be drilled at a depth of 10 or more feet. After watching the bell-hole machine bounce violently, the piers came up shorter than prescribed. . .but on solid rock.

The foundation was poured. We were amazed at how large it looked! We had water piped into the foundation (in anticipation of the restrooms, kitchen, and drinking fountains) from Hebron Water District. We were ready to begin framing up the building.

The lumber had been delivered. It was on the slab. The night before our volunteers showed up to put the framing together, it rained. We worried (shouldn't have), but it quit early so that we had a clear day in which to work. We had a large crew of men from our church (the sweet women had volunteered to care for our nutritional needs), and men from other churches that came to help. Johnny oversaw the whole deal.

Jerry, who had moved into the parsonage when we moved into our house in Carrollton, had come to help. He was holding a 2 x 4 that had to be toe-nailed into another. The rain had softened the wood so that nails just sunk in. We were using air-powered nail-guns. As Jerry held the boards in place, I shot a nail into the joint. Maybe the pressure on the gun was too high. It probably had something to do with that wet wood. Maybe both. Whatever, the nail went completely through the wood and pierced the palm of Jerry's hand! What a way for a pastor to treat a volunteer. . .and a prospect for our church! We got him to the doctor. He was fine, but didn't come to help any more.

Seeing the framing go up revived and encouraged us. People would stop by, from the adjacent road (it was always busy), to see what was going on. We worked, and we ate (the ladies did very well). We fellowshipped. It was a pragmatic worship.

The building would be a two-story edifice. As in most stick-and-brick buildings, the framing went pretty fast. We were challenged by the roof. It was so high! One of the mission volunteers showed us (for whom this was so new) how to mark the 4 x 8 sheets of decking, and how to pull them into place. He showed us how to place the clips in place in the sheet that had just been installed. Then, with the new sheet standing upright, we should take the claw end of our hammer and—as we lowered the sheet—pull with that hammer to secure the fresh sheet in place.

Tracy had just got off work, and hurried to help. We were placing a new sheet of the decking in place, using our hammers as modeled. When we lowered the sheet, one of our crew lost the grip on his hammer, and the velocity of the decking launched his hammer over the top of the roof. How fortunate that there was no one to intercept that flying hammer.

We were anxious to get the building dried in. Putting on the shingles challenged us all. We were fortunate to have a roofer to show us what to do. Getting those shingles up to the roof was not easy. We rented a sort of elevator. It was operated by a hand crank. Someone on the ground would load a bundle or so of shingles onto the platform. Then, he would crank the elevator to bring the platform up to the level of the roof. To unload the shingles, one had to step with one foot on the roof and the other on the platform. It was dicey. No one was injured, and we did get the shingles in place.

Getting the sheetrock onto the upper floor was another fun thing. We backed the delivery truck as close to the building as possible. We had left a wide opening for a window. Two men would hoist a sheet up to the opening, where another two would wrestle it on into the building.

Joe Grimes was as helpful as anyone. . .maybe more than anyone. As we would put on a sheet, Joe would check to see if we had enough stud to splice the next sheet onto. If there was not enough stud, Joe would say, "Put in a Dutchman." I learned what he meant. We would splice another 2 x 4 onto the skinny stud and have a strong hold for the next sheet to adhere to.

We did the best we could to match the bricks on the original building. We got close, but not exact. We had a very good brick mason recommended to us. Drive by that building, and you will be impressed with the quality of his work.

A major chore was installing the sewage line. Since there had been no restrooms in the original building, there was no system. We were very close to the line of the City of Carrollton. They were gracious enough to give us a tap into the city's system. We had to trench the several hundred feet from our building to that tap. . .and cross a shallow creek.

The line would be four-inch PVC. There had to be an inspection vent every 50 feet (I think). We rented a trencher to dig. Remember what I said earlier about the white rocks? Our purposed trench was filled with them! The trencher would growl and hang up. We would have to jump in with a pick and dislodge the malicious rock. When we got down to the creek, we appealed to a plumber who had his shop just down the hill in old Hebron. He agreed to donate his time and machine to trench across the creek for us. Hallelujah! The tap was much deeper than we had expected, but we made connection. What a thrill, to step into the men's restroom and flush the urinal!

Tracy was concerned that we bring our old auditorium back to glory. He envisioned how we could take out that false ceiling and restore the balconies. After what we had seen in the erection of this new building, agreeing to renovate the auditorium was not a hard sell.

We began by taking out those beautiful stained-glass windows. Tracy would have his shop build new frames for them. We would install plexiglass over the frames to protect the art. In one of our Sunday morning services, we had an unexpected visitor enter through a side door into our auditorium. He was very strange, said that a voice had told him to come into our building and throw a stone through one of our windows. After his astonishing speech, he exited through the door he had come in by. One of our men followed him out to the railroad that ran next to our church. The man had vanished! Very weird.

The old auditorium had a cheap-sort of paneling on the walls. Our plans were to remove all that old stuff and plaster the walls to receive wallpaper. We staged a day, after morning services, when our men would man a scaffold and tear out the false ceiling (that hid the balconies). As I was taking my turn, I was interrupted by a Carrollton policeman. He had been out in our parking lot watching for speeders. Some of our guys (pranksters) persuaded him to come in and arrest me for working on the Sabbath! We all (including the policeman) had a great laugh about it.

We piped water into the upper floor so that we could have hot water for our baptistry. We installed air conditioning in the attic. With the false ceiling gone, a crew—using a laser to keep the line—installed a drop-in ceiling. We suspended a cluster of speakers from the attic, to augment the sound system controlled from the balcony. A choir loft was designed. After demolishing the old ceiling, we covered the old floor with plywood to make a smooth surface for the carpet.

While all of this was either happening or waiting to happen, Luther died. Luther was one of the old members of Hebron. The family deeply wanted to have his funeral in the church. The church was, at that time, in no condition for anything. The back wall was bare sheetrock. The floor was unfinished plywood. We all agreed that we would do whatever had to be done to get the church in shape for Luther's family.

In an unusual expression of "community," we all came together to make it happen. The bare wall was painted (even though it was scheduled for paper). The floor was vacuumed and mopped. Pews that had been stored in the back, were arranged on the cleaned floor.

We all came together on one evening to bring this unfinished auditorium into the condition that Luther's family, and a large group of relatives and friends, could honor the request for that memorial service to be held in Hebron Baptist Church.

Tracy designed new doors for the front entrance of the church. The stairs to the balconies were revamped. New risers were built in the balconies (one rear, and one on each side) for seating that would allow a view to the pulpit.

All this had been quite a challenge for our older members. It seemed, to them, like a lot of change. After all was finally done, one of our sweet ladies—Polly—said, "I like what you have done to my church."

We had been living in our house on Roussillon. We were happy there, but another neighborhood was being developed between us and the church. We wanted to get into this newer neighborhood. We found a corner lot on Whitehurst. Murray was building, and worked with us on what we wanted. We moved into our house while the old house was on the market.

Our need for a more reliable car led us to an ad (I am almost sure that Catherine found it) for a 1984 Oldsmobile.

1984 Oldsmobile

By the time we got into this car, we were in our new home on White-hurst, in Carrollton. Cheryl and Brad were living in Baytown. Christi and Bob (and Travis) had moved to Coppell. We got to visit with Cheryl and Brad's kids (Matt and Amy) from time to time. To have a grandchild living close enough to see every day was an unexpected treat.

Travis had been born while Christi and Bob were living in Tara, near Richmond, Texas. He was blond and bursting with energy. They moved into Coppell, and were close enough that we got to see them regularly.

Also, at this time, Judy (Catherine's younger sister) and her husband, Bob, had moved to Flower Mound. They had just welcomed a son into their household. Since Judy was working, we kept Colton during the week.

Kirby had graduated and was living with us while he looked for a place of his own. Like many young men, Kirby was having some difficulty finding himself. . .and what God had given him with which to work.

The Oldsmobile was a very nice car. It was a four-door sedan. The color was a sort of beige and cocoa. It was a front-wheel drive with automatic transmission and air. We had the right kind of pride in it.

Our church decided to offer a Day-Care ministry to the community. We would take their kids of preschool age, give them some teaching, feed them some snacks and a simple lunch—for a half day Monday through Friday. Christi agreed to direct that program. We met several of the community because of the service we offered them.

One of the most effective things we did was our annual Vacation Bible School. We enrolled kids of the families that had come to live in North Carrollton. We really did it up big when we came to Family Night. We served hot dogs with chips and dip and drink. As incentive for the kids to learn their material, we rented a dunking booth. The deal was that, for so many tickets (awarded for participation in class), each kid would be given a throw at the booth for each ticket. The pastor—me—would sit on the seat. . .waiting to be dunked. So that no child would feel deprived, one of our men (a ready list of volunteers) would trip the seat so that the pastor—me—would splash into the water. I wore an old suit so that I would appear in proper dress and unsuspecting. Don't ask me how many times I was dunked.

The renovation of the church had turned it into an ideal setting for weddings. I should have kept better records (Catherine kept after me to do so), but I suspect that we averaged more than one a month each year following the renovation. Some summer months, we would have a wedding every weekend. We saw these weddings as opportunities to meet people. Several couples came to accept Hebron as their church home.

Somewhere in this chapter, I turned 50. I got a call that "the wedding party was at church, waiting for me." I didn't know of any planned wedding, and was flustered. As quickly as I could, I got "properly dressed" and rushed up to the church. There were several cars in the lot. My suspicions were aroused. When I entered the church, it was filled with our members. What was going on? Howard answered my questions. Catherine had arranged a special deal for my 50th. She had taken a clue from *This is Your Life* (a prominent TV show at the time), and had invited significant people from our past to come share experiences. What an effort on her part! I was more than honored. Parents were there, children were there, previous employers were there. Being her husband was more of an honor than I could describe, and here she honored me in this special way!

The church had agreed to be a church that helped start other churches. We entered into a Cooperative Agreement with The Baptist General of Texas and Denton Baptist Association to attempt a new church in a growing neighborhood in North Carrollton. Some of our good people went into that new start to give them a boost.

On the anniversary of this new church, Catherine and I were coming back from a trip to the Southern Baptist Convention in Richmond, Virginia. The final session ended on Saturday evening. I had a part of the anniversary program back in Carrollton on Sunday afternoon. We didn't do a very good job of estimating our time requirements. We ended up driving most of the night and up into the next day. We fell into bed for a less than two-hour nap before going over to the anniversary. We tried not to let any of those good people know how hard we'd had to work to get there.

We were blessed, in Hebron, to work with people who held a strong commitment to missions. We learned of an opportunity to go to a little barrio outside Laredo and help build a building that the church could meet in. Primera in Laredo would provide us a place to sleep and eat (we slept on the floors, and used their kitchen to prepare our meals).

To say it was hot is not to say enough. We sweltered, but we got our work done. It was a very gratifying experience. On a later return trip, I was privileged to baptize a convert from Rio Bravo (the barrio) in a horse trough borrowed from a cooperative hardware store.

Larry and Judy Jackson had joined us around this time. They were a most generous and hospitable family. Larry gave us one of the company cars they no longer needed. It was a little four-door compact. . .like a Plymouth Horizon. I mention that here because it was during this time that we were driving the Olds, and a very significant story goes with it.

Amy, Cheryl and Brad's daughter, had given her life to Christ, and she asked if I would come to their church (they were living then near Corpus Christi) and baptize her. Of course, we were thrilled. The baptism was scheduled for Sunday evening. Our plans were for me to preach at Hebron, then we would jump into the car Larry had given us and trust that we could get to their church in time.

We did make it. How? I can only say that grace made it possible. We had no problems on the road. The service was beautiful. We spent the night with Cheryl and Brad and drove home the next day.

Paul was one of our big-hearted members. He was ready to do what he could, when he could. He was getting a new car and wondered if we were at all interested in the 1986 Honda Accord he was getting out of. We found a buyer for our Oldsmobile, and began another chapter. . .this time in a Honda.

1986 Honda

Paul had taken really good care of the Honda. It was a four-door, four-cylinder, with cloth seats, a/c, and cruise-control. We felt blessed to have it.

Christi gave birth to Kendall at Trinity Hospital in North Carrollton. What a package of bliss!

Christi was always so good about letting us have time with the kids. We got to see Travis ride his bike (without training wheels. . .and without coasting—he pedaled as long as he was on that bike). Travis had exceptional eye-hand coordination. When he was less than three years old, he could hit a tennis ball (thrown, not rolled) with a tennis racket. We became good buds.

One year, Kirby and I added a sort of patio cover as a present for Catherine. She always loved plants, and was very good at tending them. She had transplanted so many airplane plants that we were challenged to find room for them. In this addition, we built shelves that could serve both as places for the plants to set and grow and as seating for us.

Travis and I were having a drink (likely after a rowdy set of hitting tennis balls). I was seated on one of the shelves we had built. Travis was holding his drink as he attempted to get up to the seat. In a horrific moment, he lost his balance and fell—face forward—onto the concrete floor! In was instant—and deep—hurt. His head swelled into a knot. His eye turned purple. We rushed to an emergency care center just south of us. Bob came from work. Of course, Christi was there. She was in the house with Catherine when the accident happened.

We were examined at the care center, then recommended to go on to Trinity for more intensive examination. Gratefully, Travis was not seriously hurt. As we were walking in the hospital, Travis saw himself in a mirror and said, "It looks like I have makeup."

Thinking about how that could have turned out still causes me trauma. Travis has grown into a model husband and father. What a blessing.

The church was growing and doing well. We agreed to bring on a staffer to lead our music ministry. We went to Palestine (Texas) to get Steve and his family. We thought we needed a sort of Associate Pastor, and did bring Gordon on. I look back on this time in my ministry as a time of some regret. I had allowed myself to rely too heavily upon these new staff members. Honestly, I slacked off in my passion and intensity. Coupled with my negligence was a slow-down in the economy. We began to have some budget problems. I should have been more involved, but I was not. . .to my regret. For the first time since we had been there, the church began to decline. Had I hastened the time that I should enter the next chapter of my life?

I recognized that I had concluded that period of time when my leadership at Hebron was past. I could not hold the church back, and felt I had to look for what God could now do with me. I visited with an old friend, E.B. Brooks. E.B. was director of the Church Starting Center of the BGCT. Did he know of any opportunities where I could be of benefit? Shortly, I heard back. There was an opening for a field consultant in the Central Texas area. We would have to move. I informed the church of my decision. We had a tearful goodbye service. Tammy sang, "Friends are Friends Forever." The church gave us a portrait of the building we had all worked so long and hard to develop.

I have both pride and regret as I think of Hebron. Pride, in what we were able to accomplish. Regret, in the negligence I permitted. Despite—very much so—my foolishness, God opened a door and gave me fresh, and additional, opportunity. I could still do something beneficial.

I was approved by the Convention, and began our work in May of 1993. Our territory went from Brenham to San Angelo, and north to Weatherford. I was permitted to open an office anywhere within that area. We choose Brenham.

I would need another car, one that would stand the rigors of travel the job required. I had traded an older Honda Prelude for a Mazda pickup. At the time, Reggie was selling Mazdas at a dealership in Waco. By phone, we agreed that I could make a deal with his place for a new Mazda pickup. I drove to Waco in an old black Mazda pickup. I drove to Carrollton in a new, 1993, white Mazda pickup.

I had to find a place to establish our office in Brenham. We looked and looked. Nothing was "right." Finally, someone suggested I visit with Linda at the Brenham National Bank. The Brenham National Bank was the largest building in town. We found a suite in the northwest corner of the fourth floor. Cheryl helped me find the furniture we would need to run the office. I had a desk, credenza, and chair that Mike had given me when we were still in Carrollton.

The stuff Cheryl helped me with we moved to our new space. Kirby helped me load the stuff from Mike (it was in our home in Carrollton). All that had to be carried up the elevator to our office on the fourth. The Convention provided the printer and computer for us.

I began visiting Calvary Baptist Church. Larry Embry was the pastor (for more than 30 years!). Since I knew no one in town, I asked Larry if he could help with some references for a secretary for our office. He suggested Jeanene. She worked with me until her untimely death brought on by a congenital heart condition.

While we were waiting for our house in Carrollton to sell, Catherine had to stay there. I could only get back to be with her about every other week. It was a strenuous time. The travel was demanding. . .and tiring. Eventually, I asked Brother Larry if he knew of anyone who might have a guest house that I could stay in while in town. A while later, he got back to me. Nelson and Linda White had a guest house on their place. I talked with them. They were gracious and offered me their guest house. On one of those times I was able to bring Catherine down for a visit, we stayed in Nelson and Linda's guest house.

We had to sell our house in Carrollton. It was one of those down-times when housing took a beating. When we—finally—got a contract on our house, I rented a one-bedroom apartment at Stone Hollow Apartments.

The apartment was unfurnished. I found (in the paper, I believe) a couple that was selling some furniture. They moved as the job required them to, and found it more efficient to just sell when they moved, and buy when they relocated. I bought a bed and some chairs. With minimal furniture, and a grateful expression to the Whites, I moved into that apartment (#113 I think). It took us until March to sell, and when we did, we had to bring $6,000 with us to the closing! The real-estate market was upside down. We took that much loss on the house.

Back in Carrollton, Catherine had developed a serious infection in the toe that had required surgery when she was just entering high school. After visits with several doctors, we were referred to a foot specialist. He diagnosed and prescribed surgery. Between the time we began seeking remedy and the time surgery was scheduled, we had moved into that little apartment in Brenham.

The doctor's place for the surgery was near Baylor Hospital in Dallas (not that far from The Baptist Building). We drove in from Brenham for the day surgery. Getting Catherine comfortable for the trip back was a challenge. The Mazda had seats that would recline almost to a sleeping position. We configured a cardboard box as an extended mattress, and supported her leg and foot as best we could. We did make it back to our new home. . .such as it was.

We couldn't move the stuff from our old house, in Carrollton, until we had found some place to move it to in Brenham. We looked and looked. The girls helped us look. We couldn't find anything that fit us. Finally, Catherine found an ad in the Brenham paper. A house at 2403 Valley Drive was being sold by the owners. We called for an appointment (how confident were we?). James and Nancy were wonderful to meet. They had two girls, and were building just west of town. The house was just right for us. The price was right. We signed a contract with them.

The Convention would move us from Carrollton to Brenham. We had a garage-full of "incidentals" that we had to be responsible for moving. We managed to get it all into the Mazda and the Honda. Catherine followed me in the Honda as we drove through Waco on our way to Brenham. We fit right in.

Shortly after we had gotten fully moved, we joined the friendly fellowship at Calvary Baptist Church. We met Bob and Shirley Welker at a fish-fry they offered annually for the church. We hit it off from the start. They had a beautiful place east of town in Old Washington. Bob had invented a control valve for regulating gas flow through pipelines. God blessed him with an active mind and sterling integrity. His company did well. . .and continues to do well.

I explained to Bob how we loved our fireplace. He offered me the privilege of cutting firewood at his place. We did. . .often. When the kids would come up (usually Christi and Bob's) I would take them out to Welker's place. These grandkids were introduced early to the woods. I bought a wedge and a two-pound hammer for them to learn about splitting wood. It was a festive and special event when we would go to Bob and Shirley's place.

We continued to go whenever the kids were up. At that time, Welkers had an Irish Wolfhound. Paddy was huge. . .but friendly as a pup. Petting Paddy was a novelty that the kids relished. Once (maybe her first time) Amy (then in A&M) came to visit. Paddy ran out to meet us. Amy cautiously got out of the car. Eyes wide, she said, "I'm scared." Paddy was huge but harmless.

I had the privilege of teaching Travis to drive. We were out at Welker's place. Our truck was loaded. I had introduced Travis to the standard transmission in the pickup while we were out in the woods. The road (William Penn) from the Welkers to 105 was gravel. Travis drove until we got to the highway. I remember him saying to Kendall—who was riding in the back seat—"This rocks!"

All our grandkids learned to drive a standard transmission. . .stick. What a privilege for me to teach them.

Cheryl and Brad had added to their family. Amy was their second, followed by Brandon and then James Robert (as he grew that name went from "Jim Bob" to "J.B." to "James," when he married). They were living near Corpus Christi, and Bob had received Kendall into their family and had moved to Clear Lake. Kirby was working and living in the Dallas area. Both our parents were in Highlands (Catherine's) and Baytown (mine).

Bob and Christi's house in Clear Lake was a two-story with the bedrooms upstairs. As they were getting ready for church one Sunday, Travis called out "You've just got to see Kendall!" Bob and Christi rushed to see Kendall hanging from the banisters over the stairwell! She had squeezed herself between the posts and was dangling there with a fierce grip with only one hand.

That was not Kendall's only (certainly not last) adventure. Not long afterward, she grabbed the garage door opener as it was going up. . .and rode to its conclusion!

We had work-related meetings in Dallas each month. We were able to visit with Kirby during these meetings.

It was somewhere during this time that we got a call that Daddy Ray had been transported, by emergency ambulance, to Methodist Hospital in Houston. Not knowing just what to expect, Catherine and I drove as quickly as we could into the hospital. We were devastated to learn that he had succumbed to a fatal heart attack. It was a sad trip on over to Highlands and then back home.

Catherine had a very deep attachment to her mother. She stayed with her for a while after the funeral, and made frequent trips to encourage and care. The influence of Momma Bea was very evident in Catherine.

My folks had moved from their house (one I had never lived in) to another in Plumwood (addition in Baytown).

This incident with Daddy Ray helped us realize that our folks were aging, and that we could expect more health-related issues.

It really helped, when we went to visit the girls, that they both lived in different areas of Clear Lake (not far apart).

My Dad (we all called him "PaPa" since the grandkids had come) had a severe stroke not long after Daddy Ray died. We didn't know if he could recover. Even after he came home from the hospital, he just sat with a distant (unseeing) look on his face. Mother would not consider admitting him to a nursing home. She was committed to caring for him at home. I can still see him sitting in his chair, with his cap on, in a world of his own. . .but seemingly not connected to ours.

Daddy completely recovered from that stroke! It could be nothing less than a miracle. He told of the semi-dark hours when he would repeat the name of Jesus. It was a private and real conversation. PaPa was restored to us. . .for a time.

With the number of miles I was putting on my Mazda truck, I felt I must get into a later model. I worked with Joanne at our local Toyota dealership on a red 1994 Tacoma. Just before the Staff Week that required us—each month—to go to Dallas, I was completing a trip that included Rising Star. I had completed my meeting, and started onto Highway 36 to come home, when a rain shower began wetting the road. I was coming up a gentle hill with a slight curve. I had engaged the cruise-control (later learned better), when—without any warning at all—I went into a hydroplane! I remember the truck spinning. I came back to consciousness in the front seat of a stranger's truck. He was taking me back into Rising Star for examination.

He had seen my truck spinning out of control until it came to rest, pointing in the opposite direction I had been traveling, against a fence across a deep ditch. He said I was climbing out of the ditch when he stopped (a true Good Samaritan) and picked me up.

I was alert enough to recall that I had taken my billfold out of my pocket and put it into a slot on the dash. He assured me that he had gotten my billfold and my computer.

The Rising Star emergency care center thought it best for me to be transferred to Brownwood by ambulance. Dan, who was then the Director of Mission—and a good friend, met us at the hospital. He called Catherine to assure her (I talked with her) that I was OK. As they were preparing me for the trip home (I wasn't hurt that bad, but I didn't have any transportation), Dan drove back out to the scene and did find my glasses (before contacts).

To get me home, Dan drove me to Cameron, where we met Catherine. All the pay Dan would accept was to fill his gas tank back up. Catherine drove me on home. We informed the folks in Dallas. They empathized.

I complained to Firestone that my tires were responsible for the hydroplane. They disagreed. Does it bother them that I no longer use their products?

Our reliable little Honda developed a problem with the steering mechanism. I seemed to have thought (don't know that I've learned better yet) that I could fix nearly anything. I would, at least, give it a try. I ordered the new part and backed the car into the garage to replace the steering rod (which had the reservoir for the power steering). I got the main part in, but never could get the tubing for the power steering to not leak. I kept trying. . .and it kept leaking.

We had become somewhat friendly with a couple who were growing a new church in our town. I had worked with them as a part of my assignment with BGCT. I asked George if they could use the Honda. Wouldn't be a sale, would be a gift. George agreed. It was done.

I went to the Chrysler-Dodge dealer in our town. The Stratus looked really good. We were able to close a deal. We hated to lose that Honda. It had been so faithful. Reality made this trade necessary, and so we began a new chapter with a new car.

1998 Stratus

The Stratus was a sort of golden tint. It was a four-door, front-wheel drive, with the automatic transmission on a console between the bucket front seats.

We did have a couple of accidents with this car. While backing out of our crowded garage, Catherine caught the passenger-side mirror on a step-ladder I had left out. It was a simple-enough fix. On one of her necessary trips into, or around, Houston, the car in front of her started as if to get into the traffic lane, then suddenly stopped. Catherine had accelerated, thinking she would follow that car into traffic. She rear-ended the car. No damage was apparent. The last I remember was my trip across Highway 290. The traffic from the shopping center where H-E-B sells groceries is always hectic. I was in the middle lane as a lady pulled out onto my road. She hesitated. It was too late for me to brake sufficiently enough to avoid hitting her. I saw her panicked face as she saw my car colliding with hers. Some property damage—nothing major.

I was given the opportunity to do some work with the new church at Round Top, Texas. The church was new. . .in fact, they didn't yet have a building of their own. Where they were meeting was an art gallery during the week. We had the privilege of working with Round Top on two different occasions. Lasting friendships were forged there. Just before we left, on our second time with them, the church had acquired a piece of property adjacent to the town square. I preached the message dedicating that property. I used Joshua 4:1–8, where Joshua instructed the priests to select 12 stones from the bed of the Jordan River, bring them ashore, and construct a memorial of them. That memorial would communicate, to any who venture by, what God had done for them.

As I was preaching, I was distracted (all my fault) by the fidgeting of a couple of younger boys. I wanted to say or do something, but didn't. When church was dismissed, we all went over to the property where a tent had been erected for a dedication time. Those boys I had been so bothered by were lagging back. I wanted to vent my impatience, but held off. When they finally came under the tent, they explained that they had been looking for 12 rocks to use in the dedication!

I ran into some serious trouble during the time we had this Stratus. I have, for years, had some pain in my back. I found some relief lying on the floor, using heat, stretching. The back was getting worse. Catherine was with me on one of our monthly trips to Dallas. We were in my truck (company business). I stopped in Robinson for gas. As I walked into the station to pay, Catherine was alarmed that I couldn't stand up straight. We talked about it with the kids.

Cheryl made an appointment with Dr. Sanchez, a neurosurgeon, to look at me. It was a very foggy morning as we drove into Clear Lake. Somehow, we had felt it necessary to take what we would need just in case the doctor decided to operate. When he examined me, Dr. Sanchez determined that immediate surgery was called for. At that time, there was no operating room available. We would have to wait. . .maybe until another day.

We went to get some lunch. Cheryl took us to a good restaurant. We ordered, and as we were waiting for our food, got a call from the hospital. A room had come open. Could we come, right away? We explained about the food, and rushed back to the hospital. It was close to 10:00 at night when I was operated on.

I had spinal stenosis in three vertebrae. I woke up on my back with a sort of pump attached to the wound to help with drainage. I had to stay on my back.

Christi was visiting with me when Dr. Sanchez came in to see how I was doing. Standing behind, she saw some concern on the doctor's face as he looked me over. Something was just not right. Dr. Sanchez (we came to call him by his first name, Eric), scheduled me to visit with a neurologist

(I think his name was Clark). I was released from the hospital. Cheryl had insisted that we stay with her until all this was resolved. Catherine had to drive back to Brenham to get what we needed for this extended (and unexpected) stay.

Dr. Clark (if I got his name right) said I needed additional treatment. I had something attacking my autoimmune system. I asked if this was somehow related to my spinal stenosis. I will never forget his response. "No, you have ticks and fleas." I was scheduled to visit with Dr. Goode for further treatment.

Dr. Goode amazed us with his skill. In what seemed like a very routine exam, he told us that I had Chronic Demyelinating Inflammatory Polyneuropathy (CDIP). Yes, it is rare. I don't know how I contracted it. My option was to undergo a series of treatments of massive doses of gamma-goblin. . .1,200 units per dose if my memory serves.

These treatments were very expensive and would require most of a day to receive. Because the medicine was so expensive, the lab would not mix it until I was there to receive it. I was made as comfortable as possible as that huge container of medicine slowly dripped into my system. I was attached to a mobile IV stand, so I could go to the restroom when necessary. My lunch was brought to me. Usually, we got to the hospital around 8:00 a.m. or so. It was close to 6:00 p.m. when we returned to Cheryl's.

Cheryl and Brad had vacated their master suite so that Catherine and I could sleep there. They went up to one of the bedrooms which the kids had surrendered to accommodate us. I was learning to use a walker, but had very little confidence in my legs.

At the conclusion of what we thought might be our last treatment, I stood up to go back into the main treatment room (from a trip to the restroom). Without warning, I collapsed. It was not my first. Before we left the hospital, Christi was visiting with me. I was feeling good, and stood up. . .only to crash onto the floor.

This CDIP was a formidable foe.

This latest fall, in the treatment room, was so very discouraging. I had thought I was making good progress. I had to be admitted into the hospital as a day-patient for my next treatment. My emotions had been working me over since that first fall. I had thought (hoped?) that the surgery to correct my back would fix me up. This other stuff was killing me.

I asked the kids to leave me outside, for a time, so that I could work some things out. God was very close to me. He led me to a re-study of Nehemiah. That time was therapy for me.

We were released to return home. I came back with specific instructions regarding follow-up therapy. With Catherine's help, I went back to work (I had been on sick leave since the surgery. . .which came as a complete surprise to my employers). Life in a wheelchair is a revelation. . .a humbling one.

I had a wonderfully competent therapist at our local clinic. She put me on a regimen that put me on the road to mobility. She explained that the secret to a strong back was a strong abdomen. We worked until I was able to walk without support. . .or fear. A portion of that therapy I continue to this day.

It was during this time that the girls began to notice some issues with their mother's health. Kirby, being up in Dallas, didn't see us often enough to be as aware as the girls were. Quite honestly, I was not that aware. Maybe I was too close to the problem. Maybe I was too wrapped up in my own recovery. Whatever, it marked the beginning of a very long and trying episode.

While PaPa had recovered more than the "experts" expected, he began having kidney problems. He had to begin dialysis treatments. He hated them. Daddy was always a rather private person. Sitting that long, with people punching around on him, stressed him terribly. Randy had come to live with Mom and Dad to help with transportation and care for Daddy. After one of their trips to the dialysis clinic, Daddy told Randy he wasn't going to go back. He didn't.

It wasn't much longer before Daddy died. We came from Brenham to conduct his funeral.

We were concerned about Granny (we all called Mother by that grand-parent designation). She was still mobile, but aging. Robyn, our only sister, was very concerned and began actively looking for some options. Robyn and Larry had been in Lufkin for some years. They had a house there, but considered looking for a place that had room enough for them and Granny. . .two living areas. We believe that God helped them find just such a place in Hudson (adjacent to Lufkin). It was a large house with three bedrooms, but with a separate living area with another bedroom, a small kitchen, and a full bathroom. It was ideal. We met in Baytown and helped move her stuff to the new place in Hudson.

Mother (Granny) was a fierce competitor. You did not want to play cards or dominoes with her. She soon became notorious at the Senior Citizen's Center where Robyn was director. Mother became quite adept on her computer. . .even playing cards with people over the internet! Eventually, age caught up with her, and Mother's body was brought back to Baytown where we memorialized her at Second Baptist Church.

Billy Don, Catherine's youngest brother, was living with Momma Bea after Daddy Ray's death. Billy Don was a very capable young man, but a troubled one. Somewhere along the line, he had gotten addicted to drinking. The family worked with him. Worried with him. On one of her trips to check on her mother, Catherine had to take Billy Don to a hospital on the loop in northeast Houston. They found that he had a cancer that had attacked his neck. He could not survive. How sad it was to see a young man go "before his time."

My brother, Randy, had a problem with drink also. He had been living in a facility the City of Houston had provided for people with no home. He shouldn't have had to be there. His drinking had separated him from his family. Randy had been married twice. He had children in California and in Texas. He was living with neither family.

The last time I saw Randy, he was a patient in the Harris County charity hospital. He didn't have money for the vending machine. I bought him some crackers and a Coke, prayed with him, assured him how I loved him, and drove on to an appointment in Victoria.

We learned that paramedics had to break into his room when the manager reported that he had not seen Randy is some time, and his door was locked. Randy had died from a massive heart attack. Another man who "died before his time."

I was able to resume full participation in my work. Catherine would ride with me most of the time when I would have to be in Dallas for more than just a day. She had bonded into a strong friendship with Martha Oaks, the wife of one of the men I worked with.

One of our dreams had been to go to Hawaii. By some week-trading (and, we believed, the grace of God), we were granted two weeks on two different islands in that state. We did all the "tourist stuff," toured around the big island, learned (but did not practice) the Hula, did a luau, found that the price of groceries was out-of-sight. What a long flight back home!

Matt was now in the Coast Guard. Amy, Travis, and Brandon were all in A&M. Kendall and Jim Bob (his name of preference at this time) were in Clear Lake High School. Cheryl was utilizing her gifts in decorating. Christi had gone back to school to qualify herself to teach in elementary school. Kirby was working in Dallas. Brad and Bob were doing well with their respective companies.

Brandon had met Jessica at A&M. He was tall. She was tall. . .and very smart and beautiful. How could he persuade her to become his wife? I don't know "how," but he did it. I was blessed to be able to do the weddings for four of our six grandkids. Brandon and Jessica were the first. I still get kidded about my remark when I dropped her ring. "Dadgumbit" came out before I could close my mouth (not, at all, the first time I let it run rampant). I thought it was for our ears only when Brandon had trouble getting the ring onto Jess's finger, and I said, "Spit on it." Bad Papa.

Amy and Brandon Grier were next. We wondered how we would distinguish between the Brandons. The last name, "Grier" was the answer. The reception was at a local club. One of the pictures taken was of me and Mema "dancing" (quotes to include some possible relationship to a dance). Sometime later, that picture was one the kids chose to include in the collage made to celebrate our 50th.

I was coming up on retirement. One of my concerns had been that I might not have sufficient resources to care for us after I quit working. From the time I became employed at the BGCT, I had designated as much as allowed in a retirement account. It would be a huge step of pragmatic faith.

In the course of my work, I had been blessed to meet a group of contemporary young adults. They were as concerned about compliance with The Great Commission as any disciple. Their approach was on the edge.

At their request, we cooperated with an event that expressed some of their approaches—one that would encourage participation from other young adults. The event was called "Wabi-Sabi." The name is a little beyond me, but it communicated with the people we were trying to reach. They (the locals who did the majority of planning) had rented a house. There was an "usher" who welcomed each person into the house, praying with each as he or she entered. Each room was a worship experience. Wabi-Sabi was the first time I had my feet washed. At the conclusion of the weekend, we went to a Gospel Brunch where—to my surprise—I was "roasted and toasted." It was a totally unexpected expression of appreciation and blessing upon my retirement.

The Convention provided a sort of reception, and I was awarded a plaque noting "16 years and 4 months of effective and efficient (catch words in our section of work) service." We had decided to stay in Brenham. . .it was home.

We must have had the best three kids in God's inventory. They were fully kids and engaged life with a zest. They were so considerate of us. As soon as they were old enough to recognize special days, they began making our anniversaries a very special occasion. We were served a full meal. . .with several courses. Cheryl and Christi would invent the ambiance, and design a meal accordingly. Kirby served as our maître d'. We were treated with Spanish, French, and American cuisine. When it came to our 50th, they made a very special time of it.

They reserved the Fellowship Hall at Calvary. They searched through years of pictures to make a collage. As you would expect, we had a great cake. What an honor, to live that long with such a sweet wife, and to have the best three kids to boot!

Catherine was always good about tending to our mail. Things I would normally ignore or throw away, she would look through. She noticed that our local Chrysler dealership was promoting a special sale of quality late-model cars. We went to see what they had to offer. In their inventory was a 2002 Honda Accord. We really didn't have any issues with our Stratus, but we remembered what great service we had from that other Honda, and agreed on a trade that would get us into this newer Accord.

2002 Accord

I was reluctant to go to this promotion. I thought it was another kind of gimmick. Catherine thought it a good idea, so we went. The Accord was low-mileage, white, with four doors. It had a plush, leather interior. It was a V-6 and had the deluxe accessories package. The first time she drove it, Catherine said, "It is a dream to drive." It was, all the way around, a good deal.

I had kept a pickup for firewood and the oh-so-many things you can rationalize as necessary to have a pickup. By now I had a 1994 Toyota. I had found that you just couldn't beat those little Toyota Tacomas! I had traded my Mazda for a Tacoma. . .and never went anywhere else.

Retirement had given me the opportunity to do some interim work. Larry Embry had been the pastor at Calvary for more than 30 years. When he retired, we were—all—concerned about finding just the right person to continue the good work Calvary had benefitted from these years. I was approached with the offer to serve, during this time the pastor search committee was at work, as interim pastor. I agreed that I would not permit myself to be considered for the job of full-time pastor (as if they would seriously want such an old man). We had been blessed with many fine friends in our time there (almost 20 years!). At that time, Calvary had services on Sunday morning and evening and a midweek prayer meeting.

A new pastor was called, and I was given an opportunity to serve First Baptist, Brookshire, as I had Calvary. I agreed to be in Brookshire for Sunday services (morning and evening), Wednesday (for prayer meeting) and Mondays. . .and "as needed." Catherine did not always go with me.

144

She had commitments in Brenham. When we had special occasions (such as Valentine Banquets), Catherine would be with me. I served at Brookshire for more than a year. I still relish some of the deep friendships introduced and developed there.

As mentioned earlier, Cheryl (I think Christi also) had begun to notice some issues with Catherine's health. We struggled with acceptance, and with what to do. Cheryl was with us when Dr. Leal suggested the names of a geriatric psychiatrist and a neurologist. When we visited with Dr. Tapar, she scheduled an evaluation with a team of neurologists at the Medical Center in Houston. The recommendation of the evaluating team was that Catherine was not safe to drive or cook. She was in the early stages of dementia.

It was a shock to us. It was a shock and a difficult (to say the least) adjustment for her. She couldn't understand why.

We worked with a lawyer to draw up a Power of Attorney that would give me the power to sign for her. The progressing dementia was robbing her of the ability to write her name. That first Power of Attorney was enacted in 2008.

Since I was retired, I could be home to care for her. Not that much, yet, had changed in our lives. We were still able to get about. In fact, we took a couple of cruises. I tried to be considerate about Catherine's increasing needs. We began to have our meals provided by local places. At the time, we had an Arby's here. We loved their "5 for $5." I would get us two beef sandwiches, one curly fries, and two cherry turnovers. Yummy! For breakfast, we did quick oatmeal and toast (sometimes, pancakes). It was awkward with her not being able to cook. I say I know how hard it was, but I don't really know. I do know that she kept making the adjustments her deteriorating condition demanded.

Her brother, Milton, became very ill during this time. Seems he had inherited that congestive heart condition from his parents. He was always a rather slightly-built young man. This condition made him look even more skinny.

Milton got well enough to come home, but his wife—Judy—was not well. Her death seemed a surprise. . .and untimely. Judy had precious daughters who took caring for Milton as their purpose in life.

Momma Bea was losing ground. She had been confined to the first floor of her house for months, due to her heart condition. We never heard her complain. She slept on a day-bed in the family room. Her own master suite was upstairs, but she couldn't go up there.

Buddy had moved in to help care for her. Buddy's life had been rocky. One of his own daughters seemed unable to get her life together. She had three children. Buddy felt his obligation to care for his grandchildren. He was regularly stressed.

Momma Bea eventually had to be admitted into a Baytown hospital. She was a strong woman, but the disease was wearing her down.

Everyone who knew her, loved her. One of the evening nurses stopped to visit while making her rounds. She told how that, when she was just a kid, she would come to Prince's Roller Rink. Often, she didn't have the money to get in and skate. She said that Momma Bea would invent some chore for her so that she could have the money to rent her skates. Her eyes were misty as she revisited those earlier days.

We all grieved when Momma Bea died.

Somewhere during this time, we learned that Travis, Christi and Bob's son, had met a sweet girl, Lauren, and wanted to know if I would perform their wedding ceremony. They were to be married in Allen. We had a room reserved in a motel not too far from the church. Lauren's mother was very ill. We were all hopeful—and concerned—that she would be able to witness the wedding. The whole thing was beautiful and moving. Christi helped Catherine during the ceremony.

Buddy was named the executor of Momma Bea's will. The settling of that will was very hard on all the family. Catherine's condition prohibited her from many of the family meetings (which could be testy). After too long a time, the will was settled. Someone bought that house that had become a landmark in Highlands. The proceeds were divided among the seven heirs.

All during this time, we had scheduled meetings with both Dr. Tapar and Dr. Sankar (her neurologist). The dementia was progressing at an uncomfortable rate. Dr. Tapar prescribed what medication was available. We were made to understand that the dementia was incurable. All any medicine could do was to slow the process. . .make life as comfortable as possible for as long as possible.

Brandon and Amy welcomed their second girl at Christus St. Catherine hospital in Katy. I thought I knew that hospital well. . .from my time as interim at Brookshire. We parked (Catherine was with me) and went into the hospital. Boy, were we turned around! After several attempts, we saw Brandon walking toward us. We were so relieved to see him. Little Lauren was just a doll. After our visit, we walked out to where we thought our car was parked. It was not there! We walked and walked. No car. Feeling frustrated and defeated (and ignorant), I went to security. "I have lost our car," I sheepishly confessed to the officer. He didn't make me acknowledge my ignorance. "Just get in, we'll go look for it," he said. We did, finally, find our car. It was on the other side of the hospital. We were relieved to get into it and head to Brenham. . .where we had a better knowledge of getting around.

When J.B. and Casey asked if I could do their wedding, it was another dose of grace. J.B. had grown into an exceptional young man. He and Casey had met when both were in another wedding party. That escort down the aisle led to a walk down the aisle of their own. Casey's mother had suddenly—and unexpectedly—died. Some form of leukemia, I think. Her presence was noted at the wedding.

The wedding of J.B. and Casey was the last function of our family— extended and all—that Catherine was well enough to attend. Christi sat with her. We did not attempt to involve her in the lengthy reception.

We could not leave Catherine untended. She was not really a problem, but couldn't be all-together responsible for her actions. We experimented a little with Home Health. Didn't work well. Catherine seemed to sleep more. Her appetite was not regular. We tried to find some workable routine.

I tried to have breakfast by 8:00 each morning. She would eat oatmeal well, but not every day. She liked pancakes, and so I learned how to mix and make them. We tried to take the medicine at breakfast (by now we had 12 pills to negotiate). I would help Catherine bathe every other night. She never did like a shower. We had no other real option. We had come to the time that Depends were necessary, so panties were replaced.

Bless her heart, she began complaining about pain around her bottom. I examined and noted a rather large area of scabbing. The dermatologist told us she had shingles. Medication helped her clear up. We grieved that she had this discomfort to contend with as well as the progressing dementia.

As we conferred about what to do, we agreed to begin looking at nursing homes. I had always hoped that I would never have to admit a loved one into a nursing home. It seemed I had no other option. Catherine was getting more and more difficult to care for at home. The costs of care scared us. Dr. Tapar (bless her heart) told us that there is an acceptable—and legal—way that a loved one can be made eligible for Medicaid without bankrupting the family. We began to make inquiries.

A lawyer I had used in Brookshire referred a friend who had some experience with Elder Law. When I visited (by phone) with this lady, she referred me to Wesley Wright, of Wright-Abshire. Their firm was recognized as superior and very experienced. I scheduled a visit, and Christi drove up from Clear Lake to meet me in Wesley's office.

Wesley led us through the process, and concluded that we could be qualified. We signed the necessary papers, and had the way cleared to provide Catherine whatever care she needed.

We continued to struggle at home. Cheryl was checking out nursing homes in the area (we seemed to recognize that we had no other option). She was very impressed with The Sheridan, a privately-owned facility in nearby Navasota. With Cheryl's encouragement, I went for a personal visit. The home was not typical. It was clean, smelled fresh, and the staff seemed professional. There would be room there when we realized that we would need it.

I began having more and more difficulty getting Catherine to take that load of pills every morning. Dr. Tapar okayed not taking some of them, since they really did no good—given how the disease was progressing. Even so, it was a struggle. We agreed that maybe this was the time to make the move that we all dreaded. There was room available at The Sheridan. Dr. Leal signed the necessary papers, and we scheduled the date we would move our wife and mother into a nursing home.

Cheryl and Brad came over to help us make the move. Catherine was somewhat confused about it all, but she sweetly cooperated. We loaded her recliner into the back of my truck. We had been instructed to bring eight changes of clothes. Catherine had always loved music. We got her a little radio/CD combination, and took along some of her favorite CDs.

I can't think of it now without a wave of sadness. I knew it had to be, but I couldn't be content about it. We signed all the necessary papers while Cheryl sat with her mom. She was assigned a room with Georgia (Medicaid required that residents share a room). We had brought her favorite throw (an American Flag), and settled her into bed. We left her confused but resigned. There are no words to describe the heaviness of my heart.

It was August 27, 2013. It had been six long and confusing years since we had signed that first Power of Attorney because she could no longer sign her name. I had visited with the social director about what sort of schedule would be most beneficial for Catherine's adjustment. She suggested something like every other day. It was a Saturday when we admitted her. I would come back to see her on Monday.

It was a sad reunion. When I got to The Sheridan, Catherine was slumped over in a deep sleep in a chair in the lobby. I wanted to know why. The nurse's aide explained that Georgia had to have an alarm attached that would notify staff if she got out of bed. That necessary alarm went off all during the night. Catherine could not sleep. I couldn't stand to see her in that condition. Couldn't something be done?

"Let's try another room," was their response. We moved Catherine's stuff to another room. That was a very short-term arrangement. Catherine was up all during the night going through the closets. Her dementia was getting much worse. . .and very quickly. We would have to find another arrangement. . .one that could work.

The staff at The Sheridan were very considerate. I was trying to stay with my self-imposed schedule of seeing her every other day. When I became aware of these difficulties, I alerted the staff. The social director suggested that Catherine and Neva might be a good match. We moved Catherine again. This seemed to be OK. Neva was also a victim of dementia. For some time, Neva and Catherine did well together.

On one of my visits, I met Sherlyn. Her husband was there as a resident. As we talked, the subject of frequent visits came up. I told her about my schedule. Sherlyn reacted, "It makes their day when they have a visitor." I determined, then, to see Catherine—to some degree—every day of the week.

With Catherine now in a place she would never be dismissed from— until God delivered her—I had no need for that Accord. I had my faithful 1996 Toyota Tacoma (225 thousand miles) that took me back and forth with no problems. I mentioned to James, at church, that I was wanting to sell that Accord. James is a quiet thinker. He was mulling this over. Shortly, James informed me that his son, Leslie, was needing a car. We came to an agreement, and the car that Catherine had described as a "dream" became transportation for Leslie. I held on to my Tacoma.

Travis, Christi's oldest, was concerned that I have a newer truck. He felt that the miles I was putting on this older truck made it somewhat of an issue. Travis is very keen about computers and the web. He searched and found me a 2009 Tacoma with only 37,000 miles. I followed up on his find, and purchased that 2009 Tacoma.

2009 Tacoma

The Tacoma was in Dallas. I paid for it to be delivered to me here in Brenham. It was white, with a five-speed transmission, a/c, and a metal toolbox attached in the bed. It had been very well maintained. I felt blessed. It did not have a cruise-control. I had grown so accustomed to that "luxury" that I felt I couldn't get along without it. . .especially with those daily trips to and from Navasota. Shannon had done all the service on our cars. He agreed that he would install a cruise-control for me. More later.

Travis had bought my old Tacoma. Bob and Christi drove it up to Frisco, where Travis and Lauren lived.

Kendall had moved to Austin. At work, she met a young man that was the IT Director for their company. Cameron was a graduate of the University of Michigan. He was smitten with Kendall. Their dating escalated into marriage. All the grandkids were now married.

You remember my mention of Bob and Shirley Welker? Shirley had gotten very ill. . .something about her heart. While dealing with that condition, she had a stroke that proved fatal. Bob and Shirley had retired and were permanently living on that place in Old Washington. Willian Penn, the road off 105 that leads to their place, is between Navasota and Brenham. I began stopping by (after my visit with Catherine) to have coffee with Bob. That time blossomed into a sweet relationship. It was good for Bob, as he adjusted to his grief over the loss of Shirley, and it was good for me as I struggled with the realities of our situation. That Wednesday coffee developed into a Wednesday meal. We have coffee more often now. . .not just Wednesdays.

Dementia is such a cruel and diverse affliction. While Neva was being victimized by it, she still had good communication ability. She could carry on a conversation. Sadly (and without reason), Catherine could not converse. She seemed to be able to understand, but could not express herself. I can't imagine the frustration. Catherine had been an A-student. She was very expressive in her writing. Dementia was robbing her of this ability which we had thought essential.

Although she could not express herself verbally, Catherine could express herself. By God's grace, she never lost her recognition of me. Whenever, in our daily visits, she would see me she would break into a precious smile and wrap me in a warm hug. One word that she could vocalize was "precious." I am warmed as I recall those hugs when she would kiss my neck and whisper "precious."

What seemed a good relationship between her and Neva crashed. Dementia must have been the reason. Without warning, Neva forbid Catherine to come into their room. Catherine was confused and crying. The nurse's aide was stumped. "Let's try her in a room by herself. We have that available room, and will not charge for a private room." Again, we moved. Catherine was able to adjust and stayed in that room until the Memory Unit was opened some three years later.

All during this time, we had exceptional support from our family. Cheryl, who lived in Willis (about an hour away) would usually visit at least monthly. She would call daily. Christi lived further away, in Clear Lake, and she and Bob would usually come each month. During football season, Bob and Chris would stop by on their way to College Station. Kirby, who lived in Garland, would come at least every other month.

For all the time he had lived in the Dallas area, Kirby had rented in various apartments. We are talking about 14 years or so. One day, he came home to find that his apartment had been broken into. He was determined to find a better place. . .even a house of his own. Following is a wonderful story of grace.

Kirby contacted a realtor, and they began looking. Everything was either too old, poorly located, or too expensive. They found a very promising place in old Garland. It was on the market by the original owners. They had done some expensive remodeling of a tract home. They were selling because of retirement and relocation. Kirby loved it. . .and could afford it. He signed a contract. . .and hoped.

The realtor called to say that the sellers had been offered a cash offer. Since it was cash, they had accepted that offer. Kirby was crestfallen. He had so hoped for that place. Kirby is a staunch believer in prayer. He has several tangible evidences to answered prayer. We covenanted to pray with him about this house.

The prospective buyer had a time period in which to fulfill his intentions. On the very evening before the time elapsed, the realtor called to say that the prospective cash buyer had backed out! Kirby's contract was the next best offer!

The sellers agreed to Kirby's offer and even included some provision for the older a/c unit!

Kirby has made that place a model. . .and is very happy there. Need I say how happy we are for him? I drove up to help him move from his old apartment to this new home.

As all this was happening, The Sheridan sold to a corporation. We were not happy, but had no choice but to manage as we could. Most of the staff stayed on. We really didn't see any major changes. . .although the environment was not as "homey."

We were blessed by the attention the staff gave our Catherine. She became a favorite of several of the workers. Her sweetness defeated the dementia. She enjoyed following the medics as they made their rounds dispensing medicines.

For a time, Catherine enjoyed watching the birds that flew around her window. We got a bird-feeder to attract more birds. The dementia didn't let that last.

I remembered how Catherine had loved kolaches. We got into a routine where I would bring her a cream-cheese kolache every Monday, Wednesday, and Friday. I would get to her room shortly after breakfast (sometimes she would still be in the dining room). Catherine came to expect those times, and would lift up her feet in order for me to bring her table-tray closer to her recliner. I would bring her coffee (she never seemed to like coffee before), and she would drink it (sugared and creamed). We did this every week for almost three years. We continued this even in the Memory Unit until she couldn't eat by mouth.

We had been hearing that a Memory Unit was in the works. Contractors had built a gazebo in the courtyard between the halls. We could watch the construction from Catherine's window. We were told it would be an outside area for residents of the Memory Unit. We hoped that Unit would be delayed. Catherine was doing so well in this room by herself. She couldn't help wandering about at night. The dementia had her confused about night and day. She was not aware of trespassing in other residents' rooms. She was just compelled to wander. She wore herself out walking. Seldom resting. Dementia was our enemy. . .a hated one.

We had to deal with several UTIs. She wasn't taking in enough liquid (she never did drink much). On a couple of occasions, she had to be hospitalized because of these infections.

We made it a point to celebrate special occasions. Each birthday was noted. Wedding anniversaries were celebrated. The grandkids and great-grandkids came to visit. The other residents always enjoyed those little grand-girls.

Probably as a concession to my selfishness, I had tried to keep a golf date each Friday. Robert and Kamala (whom I had met first at Round Top) and Bill (a friend and business associate) allowed me to play with them each Friday afternoon. We played at Legendary Oaks in Hempstead. We had some sort of membership there. A new owner changed the policy regarding memberships. We discussed options. The trio informed me that the best option was for them to join the Country Club in Brenham. It was closer, and would not really cost that much more. What about me? They surprised (and blessed) me by paying my membership in the club! We would continue to play each Friday, but now at Brenham.

Matt couldn't come often because of his commitments and assignments with the Coast Guard. Catherine (Mema to Matt) was always excited with these visits. Catherine and Matt had a special bond that dated back to those days when Cheryl was getting her life back together, and she and Matt were living with us in Smithville.

Our friends Peggy and Don from Fairy, Texas, were helpful to us around this time. Don had lost his mother to Alzheimer's and was very supportive as we struggled with Catherine's dementia. Peggy was so sweet to hug the last time Catherine and I visited with them, and say, "It is going to be a long time." Although the church at Agee has closed down now, Don and Peggy returned to the community and are contributing members of Fairy Baptist Church.

Work was slowly progressing on the Memory Unit. Eight rooms in Hall 3 would be closed off (by electrically-operated doors) from the other residents. Catherine, because of her wandering, would have to be moved to the Memory Unit. She would have to have a roommate. Our protests and begging were of no avail. Again, we moved.

I was given the code to open the doors into the unit. I tried to stay on the same schedule we had observed in the years before. Catherine had been placed on the "Finger-food" list. That recognized that she could not eat with utensils. I adjusted my arrival time so that I could help her eat her breakfast (often I would stay to help her with lunch before putting her down for an afternoon nap).

The dementia was really slowing her down. She still walked almost relentlessly.

I ordered a cake from H-E-B to celebrate our 60th wedding anniversary. Christi and Cheryl came to help serve. We invited all the residents and staff to celebrate with us. It was the last anniversary we celebrated together. Within just a few weeks, Catherine turned during one of her walks and the femur in her right leg broke.

The dementia had such devastating effects on us. Catherine was deprived of her speaking ability. We were forced, by this dementia, to live apart. She could no longer feed herself with utensils. Somehow, she had broken a tooth in the very front of her smile. No nerves were affected. The dentist told us that since it was causing her no pain, and that she would likely not tolerate the necessary treatment to replace it, we should just live with it. She had endured several discomforts due to UTIs. Now, she had this broken femur to endure.

X-rays confirmed that surgery would be necessary. The break had separated, so that the bone would continue to aggravate her flesh.

Catherine had been placed under the care of Hospice. The physician's assistant suggested it, and our doctor (a proven fine man) agreed. We signed the necessary papers, and felt blessed by the quality of the people who would be caring for our sweet wife, mother, and grandmother.

This break and the complications of technicalities, made it necessary to remove Catherine from Hospice care so that Medicare could cover her surgery and rehabilitation. After Rehab had affirmed that Catherine no longer was responding to their care, Hospice would come back in.

The surgery, and recovering, were an ordeal. Catherine, with her dementia progressing, could not understand what she must endure. The dementia, as mentioned before, had robbed her of speech. We were not sure how much of what we said was understood.

The necessary pre-opt procedures were difficult. She could not get comfortable. From the time she was no longer able to take her medication by mouth, getting that medication down was a challenge. Without it, her suffering would be increased. The best, it seemed so at the time, was to disguise her pills in a spoon of chocolate pudding. We hoped the anesthesia would make her more at rest.

Dr. Spah came in to explain what he would be doing. Cheryl and Brad—and Amy—came to be with us during the time. Catherine was more and more restless as the time for the operation neared.

We had learned, in the enduring of time, that singing seemed to help Catherine relax. We had sung together some of the songs she had played in the churches where a local pianist was not available. She would worship as we sang "Trust and Obey" and "Come, Thou Fount of Every Blessing." We tried singing with her as we waited in the prep room.

Dr. Spah came to us with the news that the surgery went well. He'd put a pin in her femur and screwed it into her hip. He emphasized to us how important her therapy was. We committed to doing all we could to see that she did her therapy.

We were shocked to see how restless she was following that operation. We had thought that she would sleep off that anesthesia. She rolled and tossed. We had to hold back her hands as she grasped at her catheter. We sang. . .and sang. We prayed as we sang. I don't know if we could have made the night without our kids—Cheryl and Brad, and grandkid, Amy.

We were, finally, able to persuade the staff to administer her medication some way other than a pill. She took the medicine (liquid, injected into a pocket of her cheek) with little resistance. Thankfully, this way of getting the necessary medicines down her helped her to rest.

Bob and Christi came to spend the day. We were concerned that Catherine was not eating. She would, at times, sip a little sweet tea. She wouldn't eat. Christi found that she would accept York mints. We gave her one as often as she would accept it.

The therapist got Catherine out of bed the day after surgery. She just sat in the chair beside the bed. Dr. Spah was happy with her progress. We were released in a couple of days, and returned to Golden Creek. . .with the newly prescribed meds, and the experience in administrating them.

Catherine was back in the room she had occupied before the break. Now, we began a slightly different routine. Catherine could no longer walk on her own. She was resigned to a wheelchair. When she was not in bed, she was in her wheelchair.

Paul was designing Catherine's therapy. I helped as much as I could. At first, we did some pretty basic things, like pedaling. In a short time, we were able to get Catherine on her feet. At first, she walked through a device that allowed her to hold on to bars. Next, we surrounded her with staff, and walked her down the hall. In no more than three weeks, she was able to walk all the way from the therapy room to her room.

We had been instructed to return to Dr. Spah's office two weeks after the surgery. Dr. Spah showed me the X-rays of his work. He was pleased. . .both with the results of her surgery, and the way she was responding to therapy. Six weeks later, we were back for another follow-up.

Jennie, of Encompass, had explained that when Catherine was released from therapy, Hospice would resume our care. Paul signed the release, and we were now eligible for Hospice. Jennie helped me sign the necessary papers.

Susan had been our Hospice nurse until Catherine's break. We expected that she would resume our care since we were back under Hospice. However,

Susan was on a medical leave to have surgery. We, in looking back, feel it must have been God's grace in providing Mariah as Susan's fill-in.

Almost from the first visit, Mariah noticed things we didn't. With her experience and sensitivity, she noticed how restless Catherine was (we hadn't learned that such restlessness is a part of the dying process). Mariah ordered some additional medication to help our sweetie relax. Mariah exerted her determination to be our advocate. She would not allow behavior or treatment that was not in our best interest.

Since Catherine was under Hospice care and could no longer be mobile, she was moved from the Memory Unit to a private room in Hall 2. Hospice came more regularly now. It was obvious, more to them than to us, that Catherine was well down the road to leaving mortality.

Ashley, a regional nurse with Nexion, ordered a hospitality service for us. She was a compassionate helper.

Mike was the chaplain for Encompass. We had several visits. He and I were blessed in the sharing of life experiences.

Mariah was off for the July 4 holiday. Amy, who we had met when Catherine was admitted into College Med, was standing in. I came into the room just as Amy was finishing changing Catherine. Catherine embraced me with her precious smile. Amy made comment about how my presence was a comfort to Catherine. That smile was the last conscious expression from Catherine. She fell into that terminal-sort of struggle.

Seth came as Mariah was off. Seth was both experienced and compassionate. He did what he could to prepare us for Catherine's departure from earthly life. His concern was to make her as comfortable as possible as death approached. An indication of quality in Seth was the trip he made into College Station to get some necessary medication that couldn't wait upon normal delivery.

I was on the phone with Cheryl when Catherine took her last breath. It was July 9, 2017. I called Mark, who had been so special to us, to come help. He confirmed that Catherine had just passed away.

Cheryl got to Golden Creek before the man from Memorial Oaks Funeral Home arrived. We were honored as the staff and residents formed a path for us to walk through as they held their hands aloft in respect and care.

We felt it was our obligation to provide an adequate as possible memorial service for our sweet wife (of more than 60 years) and mother.

The kids and I agreed that I should officiate the memorial service. With their help, we designed a format for the service. I would lead congregational singing. We would sing the songs that Catherine had played in those churches where her service was needed (she was never completely comfortable playing, but she never failed to volunteer when needed—her sweet spirit). Cheryl would read the obituary. I would share thoughts from Proverbs 31, a favorite of hers, regarding "An Excellent Wife." Christi would recite Psalms 23. . .as she did when in the second grade. Kirby would lead us in the Lord's Prayer. There would be no graveside.

Our ladies at Calvary did a super job of preparing for our visitation. We met people at the fellowship hall at the church. Snacks and drinks had been arranged on tables at various places in the hall. Chairs lined the walls, so that people could sit and visit.

We were encouraged by the presence of so many people. Some even drove from Dallas and Fort Worth. The presence of so many made a heavy burden more easily borne.

All the grandsons served as pallbearers.

During those years we were in Waller County, I had worked with Bob McWilliams. . .the son of Gertrude and Alton. Bob founded a monument company. I helped him set the stones in various cemeteries around the county. One morning, I got a message from Kevin McWilliams. I remembered Kevin as Bob and Sara Jean's baby boy. Bob was now dead. Kevin was running the company.

I met with Kevin to design a stone for our grave (isn't it strangely wonderful the way God works things. . .even things that are trivial in the light of the world and eternity?). Kevin's son, Deek, is working with his dad, just as Kevin worked with his. That stone stands as a perpetual witness of the sweet lady whose exhausted body lies beneath it. Like Hebrews says of Abel, Catherine's witness, although she is no longer a citizen of this world, still speaks.

I have this chapter of life that I am not fully prepared for. Living without Catherine is a challenge. . .and a difficulty. My prayer is for guidance and leadership. The Lord has brought me to this time. The wonderful life with Catherine has educated and equipped me for this uncertain future. I know that those passages from God's Word—those we regularly read together—will someday be shared together again.

I know more about myself now. I feel I know more about God. I am immersed in grace. Who knows how much longer this chapter will last?

www.ingramcontent.com/pod-product-compliance
Lightning Source LLC
LaVergne TN
LVHW052027080426
835513LV00018B/2200